WOI

Joann

METHUEN DRAMA
Bloomsbury Publishing Plc
50 Bedford Square, London, WC1B 3DP, UK
1385 Broadway, New York, NY 10018, USA
29 Earlsfort Terrace, Dublin 2, Ireland

BLOOMSBURY, METHUEN DRAMA and the Methuen
Drama logo are trademarks of Bloomsbury Publishing Plc

First published in Great Britain 2023

Cover design by Jordan Blake-Klein

A catalogue record for this book is available from the British Library.

A catalog record for this book is available from the Library of Congress.

ISBN: PB: 978-1-3504-2057-1
ePDF: 978-1-3504-2058-8
eBook: 978-1-3504-2059-5

Series: Modern Plays

Typeset by Mark Heslington Ltd, Scarborough, North Yorkshire
Printed and bound in Great Britain

To find out more about our authors and books visit
www.bloomsbury.com and sign up for our newsletters.

WORTH

By Joanne Lau

First performed at the Arcola Theatre on 7 April 2023

A New Earth Theatre and Storyhouse production
in association with Arcola Theatre

Developed under New Earth Theatre's Professional
Writers Programme funded by Esmée Fairbairn and
supported by Arts Council England

NEW EARTH

New Earth Theatre is the foremost British East and South East Asian (BESEA) theatre company in the UK. Founded in 1995 by five BESEA actors frustrated by the lack of work on offer, we set out to create theatre that reflected ourselves and others like us. Over the years the company has been award-winning in the development and presentation of work for, by and with BESEA artists and communities. We produce touring plays, innovative projects and community events across the year, deliver a unique artist development programme that nurtures BESEA talent on and off stage, and engage with audiences from all backgrounds through our work in schools, museums and universities.

*We use the term British East and South East Asian to mean people of the following descent: Brunei, Burma, Cambodia, China, East Timor, Hong Kong, Indonesia, Japan, Laos, Macau, Malaysia, Mongolia, North Korea, Philippines, Singapore, South Korea, Taiwan, Thailand, Vietnam and their diasporas. These people remain severely underrepresented in the arts in the UK.

Artistic Director   **Kumiko Mendl**
Executive Producer   **Lian Wilkinson**
Associate Producer   **Tammie Rhee**
Marketing and Digital Content Manager   **Jordan Blake-Klein**
Creative Engagement Associate   **Yuyu Wang**
Marketing Assistant   **Linh Huynh**

www.newearththeatre.org.uk
@NewEarthTheatre

Trustees
Wai Mun Yoon (chair)
Kai-Chuan Chao
Katie Elston
Maninder Gill
Nick Marchand
Richard Shannon
Kithmini Wimalasekera

www.newearththeatre.org.uk
@newearththeatre

Supported using public funding by
ARTS COUNCIL
ENGLAND

STORYHOUSE

Storyhouse is a multi-award-winning cultural charity, its home in Chester incorporates a library, theatres and a cinema.

It is one of the country's most successful arts buildings, with more than one million customer visits each year.

The new library within Storyhouse, where members of the community work alongside city librarians, boasts the longest opening hours of any UK public library. Storyhouse runs over 2,000 sessions a year for marginalised communities.

It is also a theatre producer and runs the country's most successful regional open-air theatre, in the city's Grosvenor Park and Moonlight Flicks open air cinema.

Creative Director **Suzie Henderson**
Producer **Helen Redcliffe**
Technical Manager **Andy Patterson**
Technical Stage Manager **Tommy Biglin**
Production Manager **Helen Morris**
Company Stage Manager **Suzie Foster**
Senior Technician (Lighting) **Oliver Price**
Senior Technician (Sound/AV) **Paul Davies**
Senior Technician (Stage) **Nathan Storm**
Technician LX **Jack Halliwell**
Technician **Ryan Bird**
Technician **Dan Langton**
Technician **Kelly Selvester**
Head of Sales and Marketing **Nancy Davies**
Marketing Manager **Ellie Franklin**
Marketing Assistant **Tom Weaver**
Marketing Assistant **Kate Walton**
Box Office Manager **Fiona Yates-Dutton**

Cast (in order of appearance)

Anthony Chow	**Leo Buckley**
Penny Chow	**Jennifer Lim**
Jacob Yeung	**Arthur Lee**
Ted Yeung	**Stephen Hoo**
May Wang	**Sara Chia-Jewell**

Creatives

Written by	**Joanne Lau**
Directed by	**Mingyu Lin**
Designer	**Moi Tran**
Lighting Designer	**Jai Morjaria**
Sound Designer and Composer	**Nicola T. Chang**
Movement Director	**Iskandar R. Sharazuddin**
Fight Director	**Alexandra Kataigida**
Associate Designer	**Mona Camille**
Lighting Associate	**Luca Panetta**
Sound Associate	**Murong Li**
Costume Supervisor	**Ezra Barnard**
Dramaturg	**Caroline Jester**

Production

Production Manager	**Helen Morris**
Company Stage Manager	**Suzie Foster**
Deputy Stage Manager	**Alexandra Kataigida**
Assistant Stage Manager	**Jess Senanayake**
Assistant Stage Manager	**Rose Hockaday**
Senior Stage Technician	**Nathan Storm**
LX Programmer	**Jack Halliwell**
BSL interpreter	**Deborah McLeod**
Casting Assistant	**Julia Sandiford**
Press	**Kate Morley PR**
Set Construction	**RT Scenic**
Production Work Experience	**Mavis Lin**
Production Work Experience	**Tiffany Tan**
Production Work Experience	**Jordan Yeo**
Production Work Experience	**Haley Yiu**

Special thanks to: Zachary Hing, Ashley Alymann, Phyllis Ho, Sara Houghton, Siu Hun Li, Jonathan Raggett, Rosa Escoda, Soho Theatre, Derek Man, Josh Baker, Phil Bearman, Richard Scarborough, Rachael Cowie, Jerry Cox, Jenru Wang, Ellandar Productions, Aundrea Fudge

Leo Buckley
Anthony Chow

Leo Buckley is a British actor with Japanese, British and Brazilian heritage. After studying with Step on Stage from 2012–2018 and going on to complete a Level 3 ext. course in performing arts, *WORTH* will mark his professional stage debut. Leo is also a rap artist who performs under the stage alias 'Leoscappin'.

Theatre credits include: *Oliver!* (Hampton Hill Playhouse); *Annie Get Your Gun* (Hampton Hill Playhouse); *The Merchant of Venice* (The Langdon Down Centre).

Jennifer Lim
Penny Chow

Jennifer Lim's theatre work includes: *The Key Workers Cycle – The Midwives Story* (Almeida). For Papergang Theatre: *Dreamers* (Omnibus) and *'Freedom Hi!'* (Winner – Play of the Week Vaults Festival 2020); *Into the Numbers* (Finborough); *Overheard*, *Citizens of Nowhere* for Kakilang (Southbank Centre/Edinburgh Festival and tour); *World Factory* (HOME, Manchester); *Wild Swans* (Young Vic/American Repertory Theatre); *The Good Person of Szechwan* (National Theatre).

Films include: *A Monster Calls; Hostel; I'm Not In Love; Leviathan* and *British People in the Uncertain Kingdom* short film collection; *When Evil Calls; Piercing Brightness; Code 46; Rogue Trader*. Television includes: *Strangers; Holby City; The League of Gentlemen*.

As a filmmaker, Jennifer produced and acted in *Dream of Emerald Hill* (SG50 award in Singapore) and *Night Lives* (award by Film London) which she also wrote, produced, co-directed and acted in; she was also an associate producer on *Mercutio's Dreaming: The Killing of a Chinese Actor* (commissioned by BBC Writersroom and B3 Media).

Jennifer is Artistic Director and co-founder of Moongate where she has produced *The Fu Manchu Complex* (Ovalhouse); *Forgotten* 遺忘 in co-production with New Earth Theatre (Arcola and Theatre Royal Plymouth) and *WeRNotVirus* (in co-production with Omnibus) listed in the Guardian Hottest Front Room Seats.

Arthur Lee
Jacob Yeung

Arthur Lee is a British actor of Korean descent who made his international debut on *Strike Back* (HBO) in 2015, after training at The Poor School in London.

Theatre credits include: *The King and I* (London Palladium); *The Handmaiden* (Secret Cinema) and *Diaochan* (Arts Theatre).

Screen credits include: *Stan Lee's Lucky Man* (Sky1); *Doctor Who* (BBC) and *Moonhaven* (AMC).

Game credits include: *Total War: Three Kingdoms*; *Peaky Blinders: The King's Ransom* and *Warhammer 40K: Space Marine 2*.

Stephen Hoo
Ted Yeung

Stephen Hoo is an actor and writer. He studied Theatre at The Brit School before completing his BA in Modern and Classical Chinese at SOAS, he then went on to complete the MA Theatre Lab at RADA.

Theatre includes: *Running Wild* (Chichester Festival Theatre); *Beauty and the Beast* (Oxford Playhouse); *Rapunzel* (Theatre Royal Stratford East); *The Sugar Coated Bullets of the Bourgeoisie* (Arcola/High Tide); *N**** ON THE LOTT* (Workshop, Royal Court); *Heartquake* (Royal Court); *Take Away, Cinderella* (Royal Stratford East); *Tasting Notes* (Southwark Playhouse); *Soho Streets* (Soho Theatre); *Bodega Lung-fat* (Hackney Empire Studio); *Kick Off* (Riverside Studios).

Television includes: *Hollyoaks* (C4); *Doctors* (BBC); *Vicious* (ITV); *Excluded* (BBC); *Day Of The Kamikaze* (C4).

Film includes: *Fit*; *Kick Off* and *Seven Dials* (Team Angelica Films).

Radio includes: *Whoopsie* (BBC Radio 4); *BUDDHA OF BASILDON* (BBC); *Astronaughts* (BBC).

Video games include: *James Bond* (Golden Eye); *Final Fantasy XIV* (Storm Blood); *Total War* (Three Kingdoms); *Hidden Blade*.

Sara Chia-Jewell
May Wang

Sara Chia-Jewell is a Malaysian, Chinese and English actor from Kuala Lumpur. Sara was part of the 2022 New Earth Performers Academy. WORTH marks their professional stage debut.

Theatre includes: *Caliph* (VAULT Festival); *The Object Marriage* (V&A); *Iphigenia Crash Land Falls on the Neon Shell That Was Once Her Heart (A Rave Fable)* (Edinburgh Fringe); *Her Body is a Minefield* (White Bear Theatre).

Television includes: *The Royals* (E!).

Film includes: *Shopping Channels*; *Lockerbilly*; *Cassette: Remix Edition*; *Dress Up*; *Cycling with Molly*; *LUNCH*.

Sara can also be heard in video games, including *Horizon Forbidden West* (Sony).

Joanne Lau
Writer

Joanne is a former neuroscientist and stand-up comedian. She is a writer for screen, stage and radio, and an alumni of the of the New Earth Professional Writers Programme, Sphinx 30 theatre programme, BBC Writersroom Comedy Room and BBC New Talent Hotlist. She has also been a finalist for the BAFTA Rocliffe New Writing Forum for TV Drama, Royal Court Theatre/Kudos Writing Fellowship, Cinequest Teleplay 60, Canneseries/MipTV In Development, Felix Dexter Bursary, Sitcom Mission and Funny Women Awards.

Selected television credits include: *East Mode* (Comedy Central); *Theodosia* (HBO Max/CBBC), *Music Time* (Netflix); *Big Tree City* (Netflix); *Silverpoint* (CBBC); *Ted's Top Ten* (CITV); *Specs* (Apple TV); *Gecko's Garage* (Netflix); *Class Dismissed* (CBBC).

Theatre: *The Kentucky Meat Shower* (Sphinx 30/New Earth Theatre); *Tuesday at the Library* (Moongate Productions/Omnibus Theatre); *Love by Numbers* (Little Pieces of Gold/Routledge Anthology of Short Plays with Great Roles for Women).

Radio: *Misguided Meditations* (BBC Radio 4); *Drop the Dead Panda* (BBC Radio 4); *Sketchtopia* (BBC Radio 4).

Mingyu Lin
Director

Ming is a director for stage and screen, she's a resident artist with York Theatre Royal and a reader for Traverse Theatre and the Bruntwood Prize. She was a recipient of Living Pictures' Directors' bursary 2021,

Creative Associate at Headlong and a founding member of BESEA advocacy group BEATS. Ming trained at the Royal Central School of Speech and Drama and is an alumna of the Royal Court Writers' Programme.

As a screen director she directs for *Hollyoaks* (Channel 4) and has won finalist awards for Sundance Shorts, Sci-Fi London, Enter the Pitch and ITN's Nativity Factor.

As a stage director and dramaturg she has directed the Offie nominated *Does My Bomb Look Big In This* (Soho Theatre) and dramaturged Headlong's *Corrina Corrina* (Liverpool Everyman Theatre). Selected stage directing credits include: *Onigoro Valley* (rehearsed reading, Royal Court); *Overheard* (York Theatre Royal/ Notthingham Lakeside); *Babel* (ArtsEd); *Lòng Me* (Vaults 2020); *Silently Hoping* (Vaults 2019) and *No Bond So Strong* (Mac Birmingham). In 2023 she will be directing for York Theatre Royal and Headlong's co-production of *Play for the Living in the Time of Extinction* and co-directing York Theatre Royal's *Sovereign.*

Moi Tran
Designer

Moi Tran is a multi-disciplinary artist, designer and researcher with a background in Fine Art and Design for live performance.

Set and costume design for theatre/dance/opera include: *Play for the Living in a Time of Extinction* (Barbican, UK tour); *Herring Girls* (HighTide); *The Tempest* (Shakespeare's Globe); *Henry V* (Sam Wanamaker, Headlong); *Peaky Blinders Rambert* (Birmingham Hippodrome, UK tour); *Chasing Hares* (Young Vic); *Corrina Corrina* (Everyman Liverpool, Headlong); *Baghdaddy*, *Rare Earth Mettle*, *White Pearl* (Royal Court); *Chiaroscuro*, *Meat*, *The Whiskey Taster* (Bush); *The Letters Project*, *Dear Elizabeth* (Gate); *Summer Rolls* (Park); *Under the Umbrella* (Belgrade/Tara Arts); *Raya*, *Deluge* (Hampstead); *Roundelay* (Southwark); *Tamburlaine* (Arcola, UK tour); *The Manual Oracle* (Yard Theatre); *Golden Child* (New Diorama); *Bandages* (Corn Exchange, UK tour); *A Bacchae* (Yard); *Napoli* (Leeds Playhouse); *The Jewish Wife* (BAC); *The Imperfect Pearl* (Corn Exchange/UK tour); *Falstaff* (Opera Berbiguières).

She has presented and performed her work nationally and internationally, including solo exhibitions: 'Civic Sound Archive' (PEER

London); 'I Love a Broad Margin to My Life' (Yeo Workshop, Singapore); 'Sign Chorus National Archives' (Da Nang, Vietnam); 'Sonic Signalling in Reverse' (Gothenburg Biennale Sweden); 'The Bolero Effect' (VCCA Hanoi, Vietnam); 'The Circuit' (Prague Quadrennial Festival, Czech Republic); 'The Circuit', 'Shy God – A Chorus' (SPILL International Festival, Chisenhale Dance Space) and 'SLEEP' (Live Art Development Agency London).

She holds a Master's in Fine Art, Chelsea College of Art; Bachelor of Arts, Winchester Art School and trained at Motley Design School.

Design for performance – moitran.co.uk

Art – moitran.com

Jai Marjaria
Lighting Designer

Jai trained at RADA and won the 2016 Association of Lighting Designer's ETC Award.

Recent designs include: *Othello* (National Theatre); *Graceland* (Royal Court); *Accidental Death of an Anarchist* (Lyric Hammersmith/Sheffield Theatres); *The Trials* (Donmar Warehouse); *Wuthering Heights* (St Ann's Warehouse/National Theatre/US tour/Wise Children); *My Son's a Queer (But What Can You Do?)* (Ambassadors Theatre/Garrick Theatre/Underbelly/Turbine Theatre. WhatsOnStage Award for Best Off West End Production); *Scissors* (Sheffield Theatres); *Chasing Hares* (Young Vic); *Cruise* (Duchess Theatre); *The Cherry Orchard* (The Yard/HOME); *Cherry Jezebel* (Liverpool Everyman); *House of Ife, Lava* (Bush Theatre); *Birthmarked* (Bristol Old Vic); *Big Big Sky, The Hoes* (Hampstead Theatre); *The Sorcerer's Apprentice* (Northern Stage); *Out of the Dark* (Rose Theatre Kingston); *Shuck'n'Jive, Whitewash* (Soho Theatre); *Anansi the Spider* (Unicorn Theatre); *I'll Take You to Mrs. Cole* (Complicite); *Glory* (Duke's Theatre/Red Ladder); *Cuzco* (Theatre503); *Losing Venice* (Orange Tree Theatre); *46 Beacon* (Trafalgar Studios with Rick Fisher); *Out There on Fried Meat Ridge Road* (White Bear Theatre/Trafalgar Studios 2); *Acorn* (Courtyard Theatre. Off-West End Award nomination for Best Lighting).

www.jaimorjaria.com

Nicola T. Chang
Sound Designer and Composer

Nicola T. Chang is an award-winning composer/sound designer for stage and screen. She was the composer/sound designer on the 2020/21 Old Vic 12 cohort and a current BAFTA Connect Member (Film Composer). She was a co-winner of the Evening Standard Future Theatre Fund (Audio Design) in 2021.

She currently works with various theatre and dance companies as a composer/musical director, including National Youth Theatre, British Youth Musical Theatre, National Youth Ballet, Rambert and House of Absolute. In 2021, she scored the short film *Laid*, which won Best Sci-Fi at Cannes Shorts and was an official selection at the New York Film Festival. In January 2019 she premiered her *Concerto for Ping Pong and Piano Trio* at the Queen Elizabeth Hall, which was then performed in Shanghai later in the year. In 2017, she conducted the London Film Music Orchestra playing her original soundtrack to *The Perfect Dinner*, accompanied by a live screening of the film.

Selected theatre credits include: *Top Girls* (Liverpool Everyman); *Kerry Jackson* (National Theatre); *My Neighbour Totoro* (RSC/Barbican); *For Black Boys Who Have Considered Suicide When the Hue Gets Too Heavy* (Apollo Theatre/Royal Court/New Diorama); *Of the Cut* (Young Vic); *The Ministry of Lesbian Affairs* (Soho Theatre); *Macbeth* (Leeds Playhouse); *All Mirth and No Matter* (RSC); *White Pearl* (Royal Court); *Dziady/Forefather's Eve* (Almeida Theatre); *15 Heroines* (Jermyn Street Theatre/Digital Theatre); *Miss Julie* (Chester Storyhouse); *Funeral Flowers* (Camden Roundhouse/Hackney Empire/UK tour); *Wild Goose Dreams* (Theatre Royal Bath); *Little Baby Jesus* (Orange Tree Theatre); *The King of Hell's Palace* (Hampstead Theatre); *The Death of Ophelia* (Shakespeare's Globe); *Summer Rolls* (Park Theatre); *The Tempest* (Orange Tree Theatre); *No Man's Land* (Square Chapel Halifax) and *A Hundred Words for Snow* (Arcola Theatre)

Selected film credits include: *Mei* (Sundance 2022); *Baked Beans* (2022); *Twitching* (2022); *The Fight in the Dog* (2022); *The Bicycle* (2022); *Devi* (2022); *IRL* (2021); *Laid* (2021); *Getting Away with Murder(s)* (2021); *Seafruit* (2020); *A Dose of Happiness* (2019); *Boundaries* (2019); *You Wouldn't Adam and Eve It* (2019); *Postcards from the 48%* (2018) and *The Perfect Dinner* (2017).

Iskandar R. Sharazuddin
Movement Director

Iskandar R. Sharazuddin is British-Bruneian freelance Movement Director and award winning playwright. He is an associate artist at Headlong Theatre working in community and participatory theatre and is the Joint Artistic Director of Ellandar Productions, a BESEA led company.

Selected theatre credits as Movement Director: harmony. 天人合一 (Ensemble Festival 2022 and The Pleasance); *existentialism.* (in development – Blue Elephant Theatre); *Blackout Songs* (Hampstead Theatre); *The Climbers* (as associate – Theatre by the Lake); *Così fan tutte* (English National Opera). Iskandar was the Deputy Skills, Movement, and Puppetry Director on the 2021 revival of *Satyagraha* (English National Opera/MET Opera) he was the Dance Captain on Dreamworks SKG and Global Creatures production of *How To Train Your Dragon: Live* (World and US tour).

He formerly worked in musical theatre as a performer. In 2020 he co-created *(un)written • (un)heard* a dance-theatre work for Fringe World Festival Western Australia awarded the International Dance and Physical Theatre Award and toured his movement play, *Post-Mortem*, to independent seasons in Perth, Western Australia and Adelaide Fringe.

Iskandar is a visiting lecturer and creative practitioner at Guildhall School of Music and Drama and taught a movement module for the Acting Studies BA in partnership with Central Academy of Drama, Beijing.

Alexandra Kataigida
Fight Director

As well as directing violence for stage and screen, Alexandra has developed multiple movement systems for portraying physical action in theatre in isolation.

Stage work includes: *The Apology*, *Forgotten* 遗忘 (New Earth); national tours of *Journey's End* (Theatre Reviva); *Romeo and Juliet*, *Hamlet*, *Richard II* (60 Hour Shakespeare); *Romeo and Juliet*, *Much Ado About Nothing*, *As You Like It*, *The Taming of the Shrew* (Shake-Scene Shakespeare).

As Assistant Fight Director: international tours of *Macbeth* and *Hamlet* (Icarus Theatre Collective).

Screen work includes: *Hope*, *The Promise* (Giant Squid Productions); *NightwatchMan* (Wolf Pack Productions); *Happy Graduation*, *Tsunami*, *Big House* (LFS).

Online and mixed-media productions for Shake-Scene Shakespeare, Beyond Shakespeare, 60 Hour Shakespeare, JaYo Théâtre, and The Show Must Go Online.

Mona Camille
Associate Designer

Mona Camille is a set designer with a background in architecture.

Mona's recent work and collaborations include: designs for Theatre503, Saksi Bisou at the Bloomsbury Festival 2022, Studio Goodluck Film productions, the Chinese Arts Now Festival London as well as working as an associate designer with Moi Tran on productions at the Hampstead Theatre and the Sam Wanamaker Playhouse.

Mona is also a multidisciplinary artist with recent artwork exhibited at the Seychelles Biennale of Contemporary Art 2022 and the Seychelles National Museum for the 2022 Festival Kreol, in her home country.

Luca Panetta
Lighting Associate

Luca works as a freelance lighting designer, video designer and lighting programmer. Recent lighting and video design credits include: *Edith* (The Lowry and Theatr Clwyd); If Opera's 2022 season of *La rondine*, *Il segreto di Susanna* and *Rita*; the revival of *Diary of a Somebody* (Seven Dials Playhouse) for which he was nominated for an Offie in Lighting Design; the Faction's Triple Bill of *Medea/Worn*, *Douglass* and *Duende* (Wilton's Music Hall and Stephen Joseph Theatre); Sarah Frankcom's double bill of *The Last of the Pelican Daughters* and *Education, Education, Education* (ALWF Theatre ArtsEd); *Jesus Christ Superstar* (Sainsbury Theatre), *The Wonderful World of Dissocia* (Sainsbury Theatre); *The Dream Collectors* (Derby Theatre).

Credits as associate and assistant lighting designer and relighter include: *Merchant of Venice 1936* (HOME Manchester); *Cinderella* (Stratford East); *The Apology* (Arcola Theatre, for New Earth Theatre); *Christmas Carol* (Belgrade Theatre); *Snow White* (Hull New Theatre). Luca has worked as lighting programmer with venues such as, Theatre Royal Stratford East, Hampstead Theatre, Royal & Derngate, Polka Theatre and National Theatre Live.

Luca trained at LAMDA in Productional Technical Arts for Stage and Screen.

Murong Li
Sound Associate

Murong is a sound and lighting designer trained at LAMDA, with a background in multimedia art.

Recent sound design credits include: *The Tinker* (VAULT Festival); *Pomona*, *Jumpers for Goalposts* (LAMDA).

Recent lighting design credits include: *Hedda Gabler* (Reading Rep Theatre); *Walking Cats* (VAULT Festival); *The Crocodile, hope is the last to die, Love and Money, Queens of Sheba, Miss Julie, King Charles III* (LAMDA).

Ezra Barnard
Costume Supervisor

Ezra Barnard is a multi-talented designer and maker of costumes and props with a BA in Fine Art from Chelsea School of Art and Design. They started out designing garments and fashion accessories for friends and members of the ballroom community, such as Jay Jay Revlon, and have since expanded their repertoire into theatre and the performing arts.

Ezra's most recent theatre credits include: Costume Maker: Tokyo Rose (Burnt Lemon Theatre, 2021); Wardrobe Assistant and Dresser: *A Sherlock Carol* (DEM Productions, 2022–23) and Costume Designer: *Tempest* (Wildcard Theatre Company, 2022) and *Prayers of a Hungry Ghost* (Elisabeth Gunawan and Saksi Bisou, 2023).

Helen Morris
Production Manager

Helen graduated from Bretton Hall University in 2001 with a BA honours in Theatre Design and Technology.

She worked as a theatre technician in the UK before moving to Australia in 2002 where she worked in a number of cultural and performing arts organisations including Civic Theatre (NSW, AU), Museum of Old and New Art (MONA, TAS), Capital Venue and Events (VIC, AU).

Helen is a Production Manager and has successfully produced Bendigo Writers Festival (2013–19) and Bendigo International Festival of Exploratory Music (2016–19).

Helen enjoys coordinating and managing the logistics of all the sub disciplines involved in the presentation of high-quality theatre and performing arts.

Suzie Foster
Company Stage Manager

As a freelance stage manager Suzie's theatre credits cover the Fringe (including twelve years at the Edinburgh Fringe Festival) to the West End (*One Flew Over The Cuckoo's Nest*) and everything in between. Amongst others, she has worked with Told By An Idiot and The National Theatre of Scotland, Fuel, Guy Masterson Productions/ Theatre Tours International, Central School of Speech and Drama, The Jersey Arts Centre, Polka Children's Theatre and toured extensively both nationally and internationally. In summer 2015 Suzie returned home to programme and run the opening and closing ceremonies for the NatWest Island Games XVI – Jersey 2015. For Storyhouse, she has been part of the stage management team since 2016, becoming Company Stage Manager in 2021.

She has also worked with and is a huge champion of Scene & Heard, a unique mentoring project partnering the inner-city children of Somers Town, London with volunteer theatre professionals.

Alexandra Kataigida
Deputy Stage Manager

Specialising in touring, Early Modern drama and theatrical armoury, Alexandra has also provided technical and stage management support for theatre in isolation.

For New Earth: *The Apology* (Arcola); *Under the Umbrella* (with Tamasha/Belgrade) and *Forgotten* 遗忘 (with Moongate).

At the Arcola: *The Poltergeist*, *Dinner With Groucho*, *Swipe* and *Liminal*.

Other stage work includes: *Into the Numbers* (Moongate); *Lautrec* (Hen and Chickens); *Money Heist: The Experience* (Fever); *After All These Years*, *When Love Grows Old* (Close Quarter); *Journey's End*, *Green Forms* and *Say Something Happened* (Theatre Reviva); *The Lion, the Witch and the Wardrobe* (CentreStage); *Exit the King* (Carisbrooke Castle); *Macbeth*, *Hamlet* (Icarus Theatre Collective); *Zero Down* (Theatre503); *Hood* (Soho); *iAm* (Bush); *Childsplay* (Riverside Studios) and *Prince of Denmark* (National Theatre).

Numerous in-person and online performances for Reading Early Plays, Shake-Scene Shakespeare, Beyond Shakespeare, 60 Hour Shakespeare, JaYo Théâtre, Some Kind of Theatre, Evergreen Theatre Company, The Quarantine Queens and The Show Must Go Online.

Jess Senanayake
Assistant Stage Manager

Jess trained at the Royal Central School of Speech and Drama. She is a stage manager and producer, having previously worked with Glynis Henderson Productions, Deus Ex Machina Productions and Jonathan Church Theatre Productions.

Theatre as stage manager includes: *A Sherlock Carol* (Marylebone Theatre); *DARKFIELD* (Canary Wharf Festival); *We Should All Be Dreaming* (LIFT at the Black Cultural Archives); *Ride – A New Musical* (Charing Cross Theatre); *Errol's Garden* (UK tour); *No I.D.* (Vault Festival).

Theatre as production assistant: *A Monster Calls* (UK and US tour); *Private Peaceful* (UK tour); *The Lion, The Witch and The Wardrobe* (UK tour).

Other credits include: *Dark Matter* (VAULT Festival); *Dr John Cooper Clarke; I Wanna Be Yours* (Edinburgh Playhouse); *Lavender* (Omnibus Theatre).

Jess is also a classical singer, having trained under Bertie Rice with the choir of King's College London. She has toured internationally, and performed in many of London's notable venues, including St. Paul's Cathedral, St. Martin's-in-the-Fields, and Claridge's.

Credits while training include: *Messiah, Ode for the Birthday of Queen Anne* (London Handel Festival) and *The Cloud Messenger* (Delphian Records).

Rose Hockaday
Assistant Stage Manager (London)

Rose Hockaday (she/her) is a freelance stage manager based in London.

Theatre includes: *Age Is A Feeling*, *Bedu* (Soho Theatre); *At Broken Bridge*, *No Particular Order* (Ellandar); *Antigone*, *Mites*, *Pops*, *The Ex-Boyfriend Yard Sale* (London and Toronto); *Spiderfly, Milk and Gall*, *Wolfie*, *Art of Gaman* (Theatre503); *You Only Live Forever*, *In Tents and Purposes* (Viscera Theatre); *Timmy*, *Glitter Punch*, *Sophie, Ben and Other Problems*, *How To Survive A Post-Truth Apocalypse*, *They Built It. No One Came* and *Jericho Creek* (Fledgling Theatre).

Film includes: *Heaven Knows*, *Visitors*, *Ignite*, *Pomegranate*, *Wandering Eyes*, and *Versions of Us*. As well as music videos: *Phase Me Out*, *When You're Gone* and *Saint* for artist Vérité.

arcola
theatre

Arcola Theatre was founded by Mehmet Ergen and Leyla Nazli in September 2000. Originally located in a former textile factory on Arcola Street in Dalston, in January 2011 the theatre moved to its current location in a former paint-manufacturing workshop on Ashwin Street.

Arcola Theatre produces daring, high-quality theatre in the heart of East London and beyond. We commission and premiere exciting, original works alongside rare gems of world drama and bold new productions of classics. Our socially engaged, international programme champions diversity, challenges the status quo, and keeps people returning to the building each year. Ticket prices are some of the most affordable in London. Every year, we offer 26 weeks of free rehearsal space to culturally diverse and refugee artists; our Grimeborn Festival opens up opera with contemporary stagings at affordable prices; and our Participation department creates thousands of creative opportunities for the people of Hackney and beyond. Our pioneering environmental initiatives are award-winning including The Stage Award for Sustainability and the Peter Brook Empty Space Award.

Artistic Director   **Mehmet Ergen**
Deputy Artistic Director & Executive Producer   **Leyla Nazli**
Production Coordinator   **Charlotte McShane**
Marketing Coordinator   **Millie Whittam**
Branding and Digital Coordinator   **Ashen Page**
Front of House and Operations Manager   **Catriona Tait, Carmen Keeley Foster**
Participation Manager   **Charlotte Croft**
Finance   **Steve Haygreen**
IT Department   **Oliver Brill**
Chief Technician   **Michael Paget**
Cleaner   **Milton Rodriguez**

Trustees
Andrew Cripps (chair)
Gabriel Gbadamosi
Lynne McKenzie
Abdulla Tercanli
Naz Yeni
Ben Todd

WORTH

Characters

Jacob Yeung, *43, eldest child. Charming compulsive liar with a string of ex-wives, criminal convictions, and debts.*

Penny Chow, *41, second child. Hardworking divorced mother-of-one. Human doormat and peacemaker of the family who just wants everyone to get along.*

Ted Yeung, *37, third child. A pompous, self-important pseudo-intellectual dentist obsessed with his own achievements.*

May Wang, *30, youngest child. Hyper-religious stay-at-home mother with a Doctorate in Theology and a minor in self-pity and passive aggression.*

Anthony Chow, *15,* **Penny**'s *spoiled, angry teenage son. Basically welded to his mobile phone.*

Notes

(–) at the end of a line indicates being cut off.

(. . .) at the end of a speech means it trails off. On its own it indicates a pressure or expectation to speak.

(/) marks the point where the next line should begin when one character is interrupting or speaking over another.

Act One

An open plan front room / kitchen / dining room of a 1990s-built two-up two-down.

There's a front door on one side and a staircase leading up to the bedrooms on the other.

The place is crowded with an odd clash of Chinese and British decor which have faded together over the years into a comfortable sort of harmony.

In the dining room, one dining chair has inexplicably been replaced with a cheap plastic fold-out chair. An upright piano has been squeezed against the wall.

In the living room, a shelf filled with an odd array of mismatched animal figurines fills one wall. An elliptical trainer exercise machine sits neglected in a corner. A sofa and armchair serve for seating.

Anthony *is sprawled on the armchair, headphones on, FaceTiming on his mobile.* **Penny** *struggles awkwardly down the stairs with a large portrait of a handsome Chinese woman in her 60s.*

Anthony *(to mobile)*   Well how do you think I am? My grandma's funeral's in, like, two hours.

Nah. Wha?

Yeah, we're at her house right now.

The portrait slips in **Penny**'s *grip.*

Penny   Um, Anthony?

Anthony *(to mobile)*   No, it's not haunted! She died in hospital, you idiot!

Yeah. Diabetes-related shit.

Penny   Anthony, honey?

Anthony   *WHAT* MUM?

Penny   Could you help me?

Anthony   I'M BUSY!

Penny   . . . Oh. OK.

Anthony (*to mobile*)   Nothing. Just my mum. (*Moronic laugh.*)

Penny *manages to set down the portrait, then heads to the kitchen and puts on the kettle.*

Penny   Did you want some tea?

Anthony   WHAT?!

(*To mobile.*) Dunno. My aunt and uncle wanted to like meet here first or something.

Penny   I'll make you a cup anyway. You don't have to drink it.

Anthony   WHAT?!

(*To mobile.*) Nah, she's just fussing again.

Yeah, fine. Later.

Anthony *hangs up and immediately begins texting.* **Penny** *stares thoughtfully at the portrait.*

Penny   It's not quite right, is it?

Anthony   I can't hear you over the kettle!

The kettle finishes.

Penny   The picture of your *poh poh* – It just, it doesn't quite capture who she was.

Anthony   It *is* her. That's her face.

Penny   I – I know. It's just . . . Sorry. I'm being silly.

Penny *sets down two mugs of tea on the coffee table.*

Anthony   I'm not gonna drink that.

Penny   Well, I just thought –

Anthony   If I wanted tea I would've asked for tea but I don't so I didn't!

Penny   Sorry, I just –

Anthony   God, Mum! You're so stupid sometimes, I swear!

He slaps on his headphones and cranks up some truly awful music. The lock turns. **Jacob** *enters.*

Jacob   Whoa. They cleaned this neighbourhood up good. There's a park and shit?

Penny   Jacob! You made it!

She runs over and gives him a hug. He puts up with the affection with gruff good-humour.

Jacob   Alright, alright. Don't get your makeup all over the suit.

Penny   Sorry! You've still got your key?

Jacob   Nah, just took the one she kept under the *gao gei*. Hey – What's there to eat? I'm starving.

He heads straight for the kitchen. He spots **Anthony**.

Jacob   Oh look. It's little . . . what's his name . . . uh, Andrew.

Penny   Anthony.

Jacob   Meh. Close enough. (*In Cantonese to* **Anthony**.) Hey. Don't you greet your elders?

No response from **Anthony**.

Jacob (*in Cantonese to* **Penny**)   Does he understand?

Penny (*shakes her head*)   Sorry. I tried to teach him / but –

Jacob   Oi! Don't you greet your elders? Show some respect!

Anthony *ignores him.*

Penny   Anthony, honey? Your Uncle Jacob's here. Maybe you can say hello?

Anthony *rolls his eyes.*

Anthony (*sarcastically sweet*)   Hi Uncle Jacob. How was prison?

Penny   Anthony!

Anthony *snaps back on his headphones and turns up his music.*

Jacob (*impressed*)   That little shit . . .

Penny   I'm so sorry! Please – He's not always like this.

Jacob *walks over and calmly plucks* **Anthony**'s *headphones off his ears.*

Anthony   Hey –!

Jacob   Prison was great, thanks. I shanked a guy with a sharpened toothbrush. Just missed his heart, but the hole was minty fresh. (*Blows in* **Anthony**'s *face.*)

He snaps the headphones back on **Anthony**'s *ears, and heads to the fridge, winking at* **Penny** *over* **Anthony**'s *head as he passes. She suppresses a smirk.*

Anthony *watches him go with a newfound respect and curiosity.*

Penny   Your Uncle Jacob didn't stab anyone in prison, honey. He's just teasing you.

(*To* **Jacob**.) I'm sorry. He's just really upset about *a mah*.

Jacob   Why? She was *my* mum.

Penny   Well, I mean, she – He was her only male grandchild, you know, and she – she really doted on him . . .

Jacob   She was his *grandma*. As deaths go it's like: goldfish, dog, grandparents. *After* that. That's when you get to the real shit.

Penny   Er, well, I mean –

Jacob   Penny. I'm fucking with you. Of course he's upset. His nan died! (*Laughs.*)

Penny (*weak laugh*)   Oh. Ha!

Jacob   Oh yeah, I'll get you back for the flowers and funeral stuff, yeah?

Penny   No, no, you don't have to do that.

Jacob   No. I will. I mean it this time. I'm bouncing now at this club? Real high end. It's classy.

Penny   Oh, that's / great, Jacob!

Anthony   What club?

Jacob   Forget it, Anderson. I'm not letting you in. Nice try though.

Anthony   It's Anthony. And – And I / wasn't –

Jacob   The owners are total cunts. Tried to accuse me of stealing from the door. I was like 'Prove it! You can't!'

Beat.

Plus, everyone does it. It's part of the fucking job. They were just being pricks and singling me out.

Penny   Oh.

Anthony   Why would they do that?

Jacob   'Cause they don't know what's good for them, that's why.

Anthony *looks suitably impressed with this tough guy answer and* **Jacob** *is loving the attention.*

Jacob   It's great for connections though. Met a couple of rich kids from China, right? They have this import-export business, but like with an online platform? Want me to be their UK guy. It's early stages, but like once it gets going, it's going to be serious money. Like, serious.

Penny   Right . . . Well, that sounds brilliant. I'm so happy for you.

Jacob   So, I'll pay you back. And for the other times too. Maybe even with some interest. I mean, I know it ain't easy being a single mum and all with that shitty office job.

Penny (*touched*)   Jacob . . .

Jacob   I mean, I don't have the money *now*, obviously. . .

Penny   Oh. No, of course.

Jacob   But soon.

Penny   Don't – don't worry about it. I mean, Ted's paying for most of the funeral anyway.

Jacob (*contemptuously*)   Oh. Well, in *that* case. . .

Penny (*anxious, lowers voice*)   You and – I mean, you're not still . . .?

Jacob (*cheeky wink*)   Gotta take a piss.

Jacob *disappears upstairs.* **Penny** *looks worried.*

The lock fumbles and the door opens. **Ted** *enters carrying a feminine floral suitcase that is obviously not his.*

Ted   And bend at the knee. . . and down it goes.

He sets the suitcase down.

Ah. I see you two have beat us here. Good good. Hello, Anthony.

Anthony (*mumbles*)   Hey.

Ted   'Hey'? That's how you greet your favourite uncle?

Anthony   You're so not.

Penny   Anthony!

She hugs **Ted**.

Ted (*laughs*)   He's joking!

Anthony   I'm not, actually.

Ted (*laughs*)   Uh oh! Moody teen alert!

Jacob *comes down the stairs.* **Ted** *stops laughing.*

Ted   Jacob. You're here. On time. More on time than me.

Jacob (*to* **Anthony**)   Oh. So you'll joke with Ted, but you didn't even say hi to me?

Anthony   I wasn't / joking!

Ted   He doesn't even know you.

Jacob   So? I'm his uncle. His eldest uncle. He should respect me.

May *enters and looks around with distaste.*

May   This place is exactly the same.

Penny   May!

May *shrinks away from* **Penny**'s *hug.*

Penny   Sorry! Forgot you're not a hugger. How was your flight?

May   Terrible. Eight hours in economy. The food was too salty and all the films had violence and s-e-x.

Jacob   Sex? You can just say it, you know. We're all adults. Well, except Alvin.

Anthony   *Anthony.*

May   Jacob. I didn't recognise you in that suit. You look almost . . . respectable.

Jacob   Looks designer, right? Got it made in China. There's this guy who'll do whatever design you show him. Can't tell the difference from the real thing.

Ted   Oh, you can always tell. I mean, having worn some *real* luxury tailoring, I –

Jacob   What are we even doing here? I'm starving!

Penny Anthony? Why don't you come say hello? You remember your Auntie May.

(*To* **May**.) How old was he when you left for America? Four? Five?

May *scrutinises* **Anthony** *for a second.*

May You should try antibiotics for his acne. Hello, Anthony.

Anthony *gives her the middle finger.* **May** *gasps.*

May I would never let my children be that rude!

Penny Sorry. He's just upset about *a mah.*

May Why? She was *my* mum.

Jacob Lunch! Come on, guys!

May Oh. I'm not hungry.

Jacob Well I am.

Anthony I could eat.

Jacob Atta boy.

Ted *furrows his brow at this new camaraderie between* **Anthony** *and* **Jacob**.

Ted . . . I'm not hungry either.

Jacob Well *I am*.

Penny How about I make us some tea?

May Can we make this quick? I need to check in at my hotel before the service.

Jacob You're not staying here?

May Of course not.

Jacob Then why'd you bring your case in?

May I'm not leaving my valuables in the car in this neighbourhood!

Jacob   What are you talking about? We grew up in this neighbourhood.

May (*looks pointedly at* **Jacob**)   Exactly.

Jacob   Tsch! This is the new East London. It's all craft beer and pregnant women doing yoga now. It's changed.

May   Not changed enough.

Ted   You know, you should really get a new suitcase, May. This must be terrible for your back. They've got the four wheel ones now, you know. Hard shell, 360 degree manoeuvrability. When Susan and I went to Mallorca last year, I –

May   Oh, our family doesn't believe in wheelie suitcases. We think they're immoral.

Jacob   What family? *We're* your family.

May   Robert, the girls and I.

Ted (*condescendingly amused*)   I'm sorry – immoral?

May   Oh absolutely.

Penny   Everyone in for tea? Jacob? May? Ted?

They nod but refuse to be distracted by the matter at hand.

Ted   And pray tell us, Reverend May, how exactly is a suitcase with wheels immoral?

May   Actually, it's Reverend *Doctor* now.

Jacob *yawns loudly.*

Penny   You finished your thesis! Oh, May! That's fantastic! Congratulations! Oh, I'm so proud of you!

May *shrinks from* **Penny**'s *hug.*

Penny   Sorry!

Penny *returns to the tea in the kitchen.*

Ted (*laughs*)   Doctor of what exactly?

May   Theology.

Ted   Oh that's rich. I guess anyone can call themselves 'doctor' nowadays.

May   You'd know.

Ted   I'm a dentist.

May (*drily*)   Yeah.

Jacob (*laughs*)   Burn!

A second later . . .

Anthony *laughs too.*

Ted *is extra affronted by* **Anthony** *joining in.*

Ted   Dentistry is a well-respected and –

May   A suitcase with wheels is immoral because if you're going to pack something, you should feel the weight of it, know there are consequences. That's the problem with modern society. People need to figure out what's important in their lives instead of finding easier ways to just carry around all their needless 'stuff'.

Ted   And what important things should they be carrying then?

Penny   Earl Grey? English Breakfast? Oolong?

May   The question's not *what* they should be carrying but *whom.*

Jacob (*exasperated*)   Jesus *Christ,* May . . .

May   Exactly. Carry Jesus in your heart and all of your burdens will be light.

Penny   I'll just make a pot of whatever, OK?

Ted   I don't think having Jesus in your heart is going to count for much when you go over your economy baggage allowance. (*Laughs at own joke.*)

May   And what about the baggage allowance of your soul?

Behind her, **Jacob** *mimes hanging himself, then further blowing out his brains with a gun.* **Anthony** *muffles a laugh.*

Penny   Here we go. Tea for all.

Penny   Anthony, honey? Do you want me to make something else? I think I saw some / Ribena?

Anthony   No! I didn't want anything in the first place, Mum! Stop fussing all the time! God!

He puts his headphones back on and cranks up the music.

Penny (*embarrassed*)   He isn't always like this. . .

May *grabs the teapot and starts pouring her own tea.*

Ted   So, the reason I asked you / here –

Jacob   You always pour for yourself first?

May   I don't want mine to steep too long. It's too bitter.

Jacob   You're Chinese. You're supposed to pour for your elders first. You're being disrespectful.

May (*she pours* **Jacob**'*s tea*)   Happy now?

(*She pours* **Penny**'*s tea.*) Happy now?

Penny   It's OK, May. You pour yours first.

May   No. Apparently *I'm* being disrespectful.

She says the latter at **Anthony** *as she pours* **Ted**'*s tea.*

May *finally pours her own tea, then takes a sip, making a big show of how bitter her tea tastes.*

Jacob *rolls his eyes and pulls out his mobile.*

Ted   So the reason I asked you all / here –

Anthony (*re:* **Jacob**'s *mobile*)   Whoa! Didn't those just come out last week?

Jacob   Yeah. It's a piece of shit. I might sell it.

Anthony   Can I see it?

Jacob *hands* **Anthony** *the phone.*

Penny   Honey, be careful with that.

Jacob   Ah, let the kid play. He's alright.

Ted *watches this frowning.*

Ted   You know, we just got one of those smart coffee machines at my practice. One of those ones you just put the capsule in.

Penny   Oh, those are clever, aren't they?

Ted   You and Anthony should come by! You're probably due for check-up and hygiene anyway, aren't you?

Penny   Sure, I –

Jacob   Just drink your fucking tea, May.

May   I am drinking it. It's bitter. From steeping too long.

Jacob *opens his mouth to speak, but* **Penny** *cuts in.*

Penny   You can have mine, May. I haven't touched it yet.

May   No. I'm used to it.

May *and* **Jacob** *glare at one another.*

Ted   Well, now that we're all here –

Penny   Aw! We *are* all here, aren't we? Isn't this nice?

Anthony   Mum!

Penny   I mean, obviously not the occasion, but – Come on. When was the last time we were all together like this?

Jacob *shrugs indifferently.*

Ted   Well now, you know? I'm not reall –

May (*abruptly*)   Eighteen years ago.

May's *answer is so abrupt that everyone looks at her.*

Penny   Wow. I guess it has been that long. Look at us! Marriages, jobs, kids. (*Laughs and points at herself.*) Divorce . . .

May (*at* **Jacob**)   Prison.

Jacob (*at* **May**)   America.

Ted (*obliviously*)   And successful dentist! Now before I forget – Penny, did you grab the portrait for the service? The one from the cruise.

Penny   Well, I brought it downstairs, but –

May   / Cruise?

Jacob   What cruise?

Penny *gets up and tries to move the portrait closer.*

Penny (*to* **Anthony**)   Give me a hand, honey?

Anthony *ignores her and plays on* **Jacob**'s *phone.*

Jacob (*aside to* **Anthony**)   Go help your mum.

(*To* **Ted**.) Oi. What cruise?

Anthony *gets up with no hesitation and helps his mum.*

Ted   I took *a mah* on an Alaskan cruise three, no, four years ago now. She never mentioned it?

May   *A mah* flew to Alaska?

Jacob   Tsch. That's just icebergs and shit, isn't it?

Ted   Well, actually, we saw a whale.

May   She told me she hated long haul flights.

Jacob   Wait – You went on a cruise with just the two of you?

May   Said her back was too bad to sit for that long.

Jacob   That's fucking weird, isn't it?

Anthony *nods*.

Ted   No, it wasn't just me and *a mah*! Susan was there.
Obviously.

Jacob   Must've been really romantic. Just you and your wife
. . . and *a mah*.

Penny *looks at* **Jacob** *sharply. He smiles back.*

Ted (*oblivious*)   Absolutely. My two favourite women in
the world!

May   She looks weird there.

Jacob   It's called smiling. We humans do that sometimes.

May   I meant it doesn't really look like *a mah*.

Ted   I beg your pardon? That's a professional portrait.
They just did a bit of retouching. That's what you're really
paying for isn't it? (*Snort laughs at own joke.*)

No one else laughs.

Penny   I kind of see what May means . . . but of course, I'm
happy with whatever you guys choose.

May   Isn't there one where she looks less . . .

Penny   Glam?

May   Fake.

Ted   Why would we want that?

Jacob   Who gives a fart? Just use the creepy photoshop
special. So, lunch! What we havin' then?

May   Could you not think about yourself for just five
seconds?!

Jacob   What did you say to me?

Penny   Why don't I find us some biscuits? We'll just use that photo. It's lovely. Really!

Ted   Brilliant. That's settled then. I mean – it wasn't just because of this – but I sort of had this joke in the eulogy about the cruise –

Everyone looks at **Ted**.

Ted   Well, not a 'ha ha' joke, obviously. More like a humorous anecdote. Lighten the mood. Warm the heart. Laughter through the tears and all that . . .

May   I thought I was giving the eulogy.

Everyone looks at **May**.

May   What? *I'm* the professional.

Ted   I thought Robert didn't need you to work.

May   I don't need to, but I'm still qualified! I've done lots of funerals! I actually prefer them to doing weddings.

Ted   Makes sense. You don't have to pretend to be happy at a funeral.

May (*testily*)   What do you mean?! I'm happy!

Jacob   Why didn't you guys ask me to do it?

Everyone looks at **Jacob**.

Ted   You?

Jacob *gives* **Ted** *an intimidating look.*

Anthony   Uncle Jacob *is* the oldest. It kinda makes sense.

Jacob   I knew I liked this kid.

Ted *frowns at* **Anthony** *and* **Jacob** *sharing a smile.*

Penny   May, why don't you play a song on the piano / instead?

May   NO! I am NOT playing the piano!

Everyone looks at her overreaction. She dials it back.

I haven't practiced anything.

Everyone continues to look at her.

Whatever. If it's such a big deal Ted can do the eulogy, OK? I'll just . . . lead a prayer or something.

Ted   Thank you. I –

Jacob   Oh screw this! I'm getting a kebab.

Ted   Just a moment if you please? I –

Anthony   Can I come?

Ted   Wait!

Jacob   Sure. Whatever.

Penny   Anthony, honey. I don't think –

Ted   I didn't call you all here to –

Jacob *heads to the door.*

Ted   *It's about her money!*

Jacob *freezes.*

Ted   *A mah* left a will.

Jacob *pivots back.*

Jacob   And?

Ted   Well, it's simple, really. She's divided her assets between the four of us evenly and –

Jacob   Whoa, whoa, whoa. Evenly? I'm the eldest. Shouldn't I get more?

May   How is that fair?

Jacob   How is it fair I get the same as the baby?

May   Don't call me that!

Jacob   I was out working, helping *a mah* with all of you! This is bullshit.

May   Could you please stop swearing around me?

Jacob   Oh, fuck off.

Anthony *laughs.*

Jacob   What are you laughing at?

Anthony *shuts up.*

Penny   Well, the will is what *a mah* wanted, so I guess we should honour that, right?

Jacob   The fuck we will!

As they argue, **Ted** *silently takes out his wallet, and counts out £44. He divides it up between them, a pound coin, and £10 note each.*

May   What are you doing?

Ted   Dividing her money. Forty-four pounds, so divided by four is eleven each. Excuse the change.

Penny   . . . Forty-four pounds?

Jacob   What you on about?

Ted   Forty-four pounds. That's how much money *a mah* had between her accounts.

Anthony   Whoa.

Penny   I don't understand. What are you saying?

Ted *pulls out a folded bank statement from his pocket.* **Jacob** *and* **May** *snatch at it.* **Jacob** *wins.*

Jacob   The fuck?! Where's the rest?

May   Let me see! (*Reading.*) Well, that can't be right. Maybe she had some accounts we don't know about? Or –

Jacob   Where's the rest of the fucking money?

Ted   That's it. That's all any of us are getting. You're looking at it.

Jacob   You think this is funny?

Ted   No. And I don't know why you're so upset. It's not like you were the one giving her money every month.

Jacob   Well, if you were then where did it go?!

May   Stop yelling!

Penny   Wait – I – I was giving her money too. This doesn't make sense.

Ted   I looked. I looked for other accounts, assets, banking errors . . .

May   Well where did you guys pay her every month? Do you have an account number or something?

Ted   I gave her cash.

Penny   Same. It's what she wanted.

May   Well, where is it?!

Jacob   Yeah, where's the fucking money, Ted?!

Ted   I DON'T KNOW! I DON'T KNOW I DON'T KNOW I DON'T KNOW!

The rest of the siblings shut up at his outburst.

Ted   I don't know, OK? I must've given her thousands! I just – I don't know.

Penny   It's OK, Ted. We're all here. We'll figure this out together.

May *takes her eleven pounds and tidies it away into her purse with a snap.*

May   Well, at least we can sell this place. I mean, it's never going to be nice by American standards, but it must be worth something.

Jacob   Shit. Right. I forgot about the house. Phew! I thought she'd totally fucked us over.

Ted   Actually . . .

Penny   / Ted?

May   What? What is it?

Jacob   Don't say it. Don't even fucking say it.

Ted *takes out another envelope from his pocket.* **May** *snatches it from him and reads.*

May   Repossession?!

Anthony   What does that mean?

Everyone speaks over one another.

Penny   / But what about the money we were giving her?

May   / How could she lose the house?

Jacob   The fuck are you talking about?! What do you mean she lost it?! We're standing in it right now!

Ted   She was broke, OK?! *A mah* didn't have enough to pay off the mortgage and the bank took it back!

Long beat as they digest this news.

Jacob   Fuck!

Penny   So this house – the one we're in right now – has been . . .

Ted   Foreclosed.

May   Are we trespassing?!

Ted   Well, I mean, *technically* yes, but –

Penny   Oh, Ted!

Ted   But I figured if our keys still fit, we're not breaking in *per se* . . .

Penny   / Ted!

May   You lied to us! You tricked us into breaking the law!

Ted   No! I mean, yes! I mean, what are they going to do
– our mum just died!

Jacob   Playing the dead mum card. Nice.

Ted   Look. I'm sorry to have to be the bearer of bad news –

Jacob   No you're not. You're smiling.

Ted   What? Oh, I assure you, I am getting no joy from –

Jacob   You are! You're fucking getting off on this, aren't you?

Ted   What? No!

Jacob   You so are. You're loving this! The fact that you
knew something and we didn't. You live for this shit.

Ted   I don't!

Jacob   I'll bet your little nerdy prick is just rock hard at the
thought that you were the person who got to 'Ted-splain'
this all to us.

(*To* **May** *and* **Penny**.) You should've heard his voice when he
called from the hospital to tell me *a mah* was dead. I shoulda
charged him by the minute.

Ted   Don't be disgusting! I –

Penny   But wait. I still don't understand –

Jacob   Say it again, Pen. He *loves* it when you talk dirty to
him.

Ted   Shut up! No I don't!

Penny   But how did she not have enough money? We were
both giving her cash and – and she never said a word!

Ted (*sighs*)   She had an 'endowment mortgage'.

May   A what?

Jacob (*in breathy voice*)   Yes, Ted. Why don't you explain it to us?

Ted   Not if you're going to be like that!

Anthony   Just google it! Seriously. Old people. (*Taps at phone.*) How do you spell endowelment?

May   Is that what he said?

Penny   I heard annulment mortgage.

Anthony   I-N . . . O?

Ted *tries to resist, but can't help himself from blurting:*

Ted   I said ENDOWMENT! ENDOWMENT MORTGAGE! It means she paid interest only on the capital, and the payout from the endowment policy was supposed to cover the mortgage with more besides, but it didn't. Just like it didn't for thousands of other people in the eighties and nineties.

As **Ted** *talks,* **Jacob** *holds his hand over* **Ted**'s *crotch and lifts a finger, miming an erection.*

Jacob *makes an escalating whistle noise.*

Ted *swats his hand away.*

Ted   Jacob, I swear to God!

May   Just ignore him! Go on.

Ted   Well, while other people remortgaged, downsized, or – stop it, Jacob! – came up with another repayment plan – Jacob! – *a mah* ignored all the notices and advice, went well past the window for – stop that! – for making any complaints, and long story short she got a £20,000 payout which wasn't enough to pay off the £40,000 outstanding at the end of her mortgage term last year – ah! She then ignored all the legal notices and court dates and then, well, she died. JACOB!

Jacob *laughs.*

Penny So it's . . . really gone. All of it.

The siblings look around them at their childhood home.

May How could you guys let this happen?!

Ted 'You guys'? I'm sorry, but she was your mother too.

May I don't even live in this country!

Jacob It's not on us you moved to fucking Vermont or wherever.

May Virginia! I can't believe you don't even know that.

Jacob Well, like you know where I live.

May Elephant and Castle.

Jacob . . . Well, you have to admit it's got a catchier name.

Anthony But it's not fair! This is *poh poh's* stuff! Mum!

Penny *is too lost in her own thoughts to hear him.*

Penny I just – I don't understand why she didn't say something to us.

Ted What good would that have done? I was already giving her money every month. Loads.

Penny So was I! . . . Well, less.

May Well then where did it all go?

Beat.

May, **Ted** *and* **Penny** *look at* **Jacob**. **Anthony** *follows their gaze.*

Jacob OK, I mean, yeah, I borrowed some money. Sure, but I didn't take *all* of it. I mean, we're talking thousands, right?

May Well then, where's the money? She had the payout from the policy too, right? I mean, thousands of pounds don't just disappear!

They think about this.

This can't be right. I'm gonna talk to the bank myself.
They –

Jacob *slams his fist against the wall, making everyone jump.*

Jacob   FUCK! Are you fucking kidding me? What fucking
difference is it going to make if *you* go talk to them, May?!
You honestly think you're *so* special that somehow *you*
talking to them is gonna fix all this?!

Everyone is too startled to reply.

This whole thing is giving me the runs. I gotta go take a shit.

He storms up the stairs. A door slams.

Ted   Well, I think he took that rather well.

May (*on the verge of tears*)   I don't think I'm special. Why
would he say that? I'm the last person in *the world* who would
say they were special.

Penny   Of course, May.

May   But – But you have to admit I put up with a lot from
this family.

Penny *and* **Ted** *exchange a look. This infuriates* **May**.

May   You've all been attacking me ever since I stepped
through that door!

Ted   I beg your pardon? When did any of us do that?

May   You were making fun of my faith.

Ted   I was telling you to get a new suitcase. And what did
Penny do? She hasn't said a word.

May   Well, she didn't stop you. And Anthony was being
rude.

Anthony   The fuck? Why am I in this?

May   There. You see? Swearing at me.

Anthony   I wasn't swearing AT you!

May   You shouldn't be swearing at all!

Penny   Honey, just apologise to your Auntie May. Please?

Anthony   No way! I don't owe any of you anything! I've got nothing to do with any of you and your dramatic bullshit! I'm out.

He stomps upstairs.

May   You're just going to let your son talk to me like that?

Penny   I'm sorry. He's just –

Ted   I don't know that having an influence like Jacob in his life is a good thing.

Penny   He's just upset.

May   Well what about me? *I'm* upset! You guys just don't get it do you? How hard this is for me?

Ted   It's hard on all of us. We're about to go to our mother's funeral.

May   But it's extra hard on me! Being *here*. This house.

Ted   You think it's not hard for us? Stop being such a baby.

May   Don't call me that!

Penny   He doesn't mean anything by it. It's just, well, you're the youngest.

May   That's exactly why this is worse for me than all of you! You were all old enough to leave, but I wasn't. I was stuck here for another seven years with her! Alone!

Ted   Penny and I were practically here every day.

May   No you weren't!

Ted   Ha! Like *a mah* was going to pay for a babysitter.

Penny   We tried to be around, May. It's just – it was hard on us too.

May   Well, at least you had the option of leaving. I didn't!
THIS was my home. This house! And now I'm back and it's
like the last ten years in America meant nothing.
Everything's the same. This house! This family!

(*At portrait.*) I mean, just look at her!

Penny   Shh. It's OK.

Penny *goes to hug* **May** *but remembers at the last minute to pat her
awkwardly on the shoulder instead.*

May   She did this on purpose.

Ted   What? Die broke and homeless?

May   Yes! Just to – just to ruin my life even after she's gone.

Penny   I'm sure that's not true.

Ted (*sarcastic*)   Ruin *your* life. Because this only affects you.

May   I needed that money, you know.

Ted   I thought you and Robert were fine for cash. I mean,
it's not like you have to work, is it?

May   Not for me! For Kelly and Emma. Universities in
America aren't cheap, you know.

Penny   You've got plenty of time before you need to start
worrying about that, don't you?

May   Emma's nearly *three*. And it's the principle! *A mah*
owes me that money. For what she put me through.

May *looks at the plastic fold-out chair at the dining table.*

Ted   Oh. Is that what this is all about? It's been how long,
May?

May   Eighteen years.

Ted   Precisely. Get over it already.

Penny   What's been eighteen years? What are you guys
talking about?

May   How can you just tell me to get over something like *that*?!

Ted   Because that was nothing. *A mah* did that kind of stuff all the time. What about actual money? You know Penny and I used to have to pay our pay cheques directly into her account? Oh yes. Then she'd give *us* an allowance. Of our own money! I mean, thank goodness she started asking for cash.

Penny   Well, I –

Ted   Didn't trust banks, you see. Convinced they were ripping her off. Projection. That's what I call that.

Penny   But she –

May   Who cares about money? What about the emotional pain of what I went through?

Ted   *You* care! I mean, isn't that what this is all about? The cash?

May   No! . . . Well, I mean –

Penny (*realisation dawning*)   The cash. . .

Ted   And what about all the gifts I bought her over the years? The jewellery, the holidays. . .

Penny   Guys?

Ted   That – that portrait! I paid for that! Me!

Penny   Guys, the cash. I think I know where the money –

Ted   My success paid for all of this! Mine! And she'd just hoard it all up in her little biscuit tins and margarine tubs like some paranoid squirrel!

Penny   / It's –

May   What are you even talking about? Why would *a mah* do that?

Ted   Oh, it's just one of those older generation immigrant things – They don't trust banks. I mean, sort of ironic given her mortgage fiasco.

May   'One of those older generation immigrant things'? You're such a racist!

Ted   I am not a racist. I subscribe to *The Guardian*!

Penny   I don't think / that's right, I –

Ted   Well, obviously statistically some racists must subscribe to *The Guardian* . . . but I'm not making this up! My orthodontist friend Rizwan – great guy – said his nan was exactly the same. Ferrero Rocher boxes of gold and jewellery all in the attic.

Penny   Guys, listen to / yourselves.

May   It's not just immigrants! I've heard of other people doing it too.

Ted   Well, see? That just proves my point. It's a thing.

Penny   Guys, please! Just – just listen! What if . . . what if *a mah* knew she couldn't pay off the house, and – and she took everything out so they wouldn't seize it?

May   What do you mean?

Penny   Maybe she didn't want everything she'd worked so hard for to be taken from her so – so she did what she normally does . . .

Ted (*gasp!*)   Squeaking squirrels . . . It's here! It's here isn't it?

May   What's here?

Ted   Everything! It's here! In the house!

Penny   Yeah, that's what I was –

May (*realisation dawns*)   Of course!

Ted   Well, thank goodness I figured that out, eh? Could've been a disaster!

Penny *gives him a look but says nothing.*

May (*laughs*)   So we were stressing over nothing!

Ted (*laughs*)   I mean, what a relief! I was like – (*Makes a panic face.*) Eek!

May (*laughs, makes a panic face back*)   Ack!

Ted *and* **May** *exchange faces and laughs until it peters out.* **Penny** *watches them, waiting for the proverbial penny to drop. It does.*

May   Wait. Where's Jacob?

Penny (*patiently*)   The bathroom.

Ted   How long has he –?

A crash is heard upstairs.

Ted   That sneaky / bastard!

May   He knew!

Ted *and* **May** *race for the stairs.*

Penny (*to portrait*)   What have you done?

Ted *and* **May** *almost run into* **Anthony** *barrelling down the stairs.*

Anthony   MUM! Uncle Jacob's gone crazy! He's –

Jacob   SHH! Shut up! Just –

Jacob *chases* **Anthony**, *but freezes when he sees everyone staring up at him.*

Jacob   Oh. Hey guys. Uh. I think I'll just see you guys there. My stomach's acting up? I'm gonna go grab a –

He takes another step, and something falls out the bottom of his trouser leg.

May   Is that . . . *a mah's* watch?

Jacob   No.

As he bends down, a handful of cash and assorted jewellery falls out of his pocket.

Jacob (*swears in Cantonese*)   Puk gai.

Anthony   That's *poh poh's* stuff!

Jacob *makes a dash for the door.* **Ted** *and* **May** *block him.*

Penny   / Stop! Someone's going to get hurt!

Jacob   Get out of my way!

Ted   Stop him!

Anthony   Why are you taking *poh poh's* stuff?

Jacob   Hey. It's not stealing if it's from a dead person.

Ted   It bloody well is!

May   Look at all this! Is that her *ring*?

Ted   How did you know? How did you know where to look?

Jacob   How did you guys not? She talked about hiding her stuff all the time.

May   No she didn't.

Penny   She kind of did.

Ted   She didn't say *where*.

Jacob   She did to me.

Ted   She – Wh- Why would she tell *you*?

Jacob   Because she loved me more.

Ted   Stop joking around.

May   Where's the rest?

Jacob   What do you mean where's the rest? That's all of it.

May   Of course there's more. Ted said she cashed in her policy. She had to have had at least twenty thousand from that.

Jacob   Whoa, whoa. Hold up. 20K? In cash?

Anthony (*indicating the pile on the floor*)   How much is that?

May *starts counting it.*

Ted (*to* **Jacob**)   Where is it?

Jacob   Hey, I didn't know about no 20K cash. That's all that was upstairs, OK? I swear! Search me if you want! I will bend over and cough, OK?

Ted   Jacob, if it's been up your arse, you can keep it.

May (*finishes counting*)   There's about two grand in cash, plus other random jewellery and things.

Anthony   So that means there's still £18,000 in cash somewhere in this house?

Ted   At least.

Everyone stares at the now seemingly-measly amount of cash and jewellery on the floor.

Penny   We don't know that, and even if we did, she might not have wanted us to have that money. I mean, she would've said *something*, right?

No one looks convinced by this.

May   I'm telling you guys she did this on purpose. She always had a reason. For everything.

Ted   It does seem a waste to not even look. I mean, if it's here and we leave it, it'll be gone. Forever.

Penny   But if she didn't want us to –

Jacob   You wouldn't want all of *a mah*'s hard earned cash to go to waste, would you, Pen?

Penny   No, but, I mean, what exactly are you guys proposing here?

May   We'll just have to search the entire house.

Anthony   What about *poh poh's* funeral?

Jacob   Well, I'd rather miss that than eighteen grand, wouldn't you, Adam?

Ted (*checking his watch*)   We've got time. Plus, it's entirely plausible they could change the locks while we're all at the service . . .

Beat.

Penny   See? I mean, is this legal? It's not even her house anymore! And we really shouldn't be late for *a mah's* funeral, right? . . . Right?

Jacob   I'm in.

May   Me too.

Ted   It makes sense.

Jacob   Hey. We're doing this with or without you, Pen.

May (*at* **Anthony**)   But it'd be faster if *all* of us were searching.

Anthony   No way. You're all crazy.

He flops on the armchair. **Jacob** *eyes him suspiciously.*

Jacob   Penny, think about your son. I mean, wouldn't *a mah* want her money to go to family instead of strangers? (*In Cantonese.*) We have to look out for our own.

Ted   I can't believe I'm saying this, but he's got a point, Pen.

Penny *looks at her son.*

Penny (*sighs*)   Fine.

Jacob   Whoop! Let the great treasure hunt begin!

Interval.

Act Two

Everyone looks impatient as **Ted** *delivers some ground rules.*

Ted   If we're going to search this house, we're not going to act like a bunch of animals. We're going to have / rules.

Jacob   Tsch! Who put him in charge?

Ted   First rule: Whatever we find, we split. Evenly. Second rule –

Jacob   No fucking way! Finders keepers!

Penny   We have to share. It's what *a mah* would've wanted.

May   No. Us fighting. *That's* what she wanted.

Ted   Second rule: No fighting. Agreed?

The others make noises of unenthusiastic agreement and nod.

Ted   OK then. Three . . . Two . . . JACOB!

Jacob *has already begun.*

Ted   Oh, what the hell. Go!

They all rifle through the house, turning things over, opening drawers, and generally making a mess.

Jacob   Where's the cash?! I just keep finding fucking toenail clippers!

Jacob *dumps a shoe box onto the ground in frustration.*

Ted   Hey! My awards from school! Maths Olympiad, chemistry . . . Where were –

Jacob   Argh! There's nothing here! Just a bunch of stupid diet recipes. And a fucking toenail clipper!

May   There's nothing valuable over here either.

Ted *tenderly picks up each of his old awards.*

Ted   I worked really hard for these. . .

Jacob   Pen?

Penny   Um. I think I found her drink stash?

She holds up a half-empty bottle of baijiu.

Jacob   Sweet!

Jacob *grabs the bottle, takes a swig, and pushes* **Penny** *away to search through the rest of the booze.*

May   Why does she have so many biscuit tins? I don't even remember us eating that many biscuits.

Penny (*jokes*)   I guess we know why she was diabetic now, huh?

May   How can you joke at a time like this?

Penny   Sorry, I was just –

May (*opens biscuit tin*)   Buttons, screws and . . . a toenail clipper.

Jacob *finds a thick envelope. He quickly pockets it.*

May   Hey. What was that?

Jacob   What was what?

Anthony   You put something in your pocket – I saw it too!

May   He found the cash!

Jacob   What? No I didn't.

Jacob *scurries to the sofa and plops down. In his haste, he steps on* **Ted**'s *box of awards and crushes it.* **Ted** *stares at his ruined awards. It's the last straw.*

Ted   That's IT! TIME OUT!

Ted *angrily stalks over to* **Jacob**.

Ted   Where is it?! I know you found something!

Jacob   Hm? What? I'm tired. I just felt like lying down for a bit.

Ted   Stop it!

Jacob   Stop what? I don't know what you're talking about, mate.

Ted   Stop it! I know you have it!

Jacob   You're so *paranoid*.

Ted *and* **May** *start trying to frisk* **Jacob**.

Jacob   Oi! Buy me a drink first! Hey! Get off of me! Ow!

Penny   Don't! Someone's gonna get hurt!

Anthony *pulls out his phone and starts recording.*

Anthony   This is awesome . . .

Jacob   Ow! No!

(*Spots* **Anthony**.) Hey! Put that away you little shit!

The envelope falls out of **Jacob**'s *pocket.*

May   / There!

Jacob   No!

Ted   I've got him!

Ted *holds* **Jacob**'s *foot as* **May** *grabs the envelope.* **Jacob** *wriggles free, leaving his sock in* **Ted**'s *hand.* **Ted** *throws it at* **Jacob**, *but it ends up hitting* **Penny** *in the face.*

Penny   Ack! Gross!

She stumbles back onto **Jacob** *who falls over.*

Jacob   Agh!!!

Penny   Sorry!

May *opens the envelope.*

Ted   May! May's got it!

Ted *tries to climb over the sofa to get to* **May**, *but* **Jacob** *leaps onto him. They roll and flop over the sofa.* **Ted** *ends up smacking his foot right into* **May**'s *face.*

May   OWW!

Everyone freezes. **May** *clasps her hands over her nose in pain.*

Penny   May! Are you OK?

May (*through her hands*)   No! I think he broke my nose!

Ted   I didn't – I didn't mean to – I –

Jacob (*to* **Ted**)   *Aiyah* . . . Now you've done it.

Penny   Let's have a look?

Penny *gently tries to nudge* **May**'s *hands away.*

May (*through her hands*)   OW! DON'T TOUCH ME!

Penny   Sorry!

Jacob   Way to break her face, Ted.

Ted   If there's any dental damage, I – I know a great cosmetic dentist and –

May   It's not my mouth! It's my nose, you idiot!

Jacob   That's a shame.

Ted *elbows him.* **Jacob** *elbows back.*

Penny   C'mon. Let's have a look.

May   Is it bad?

Penny (*lying*)   No.

May *turns around to the rest of the room. Her face is a mess of blood.*

Ted   / Oh bollocks . . .

Anthony   Whoa.

Anthony *snaps a photo on his phone.*

Jacob *takes the opportunity while they're all distracted to casually move closer to the envelope* **May** *has dropped. He picks it up.*

May   Give me your phone. I want to – (*Shriek!*)

The shriek startles **Jacob** *and he drops the envelope. Cash spills out. The other siblings spin around to look at him.*

Jacob   Oops.

Ted   You bastard!

Jacob   Hey! Look! It's only – It's only a grand . . . That's barely any when you think about the rest.

Beat.

I mean, you can't blame a guy for trying, can you?

May *bursts into tears.*

Penny *looks unsure whether to hug* **May** *or not. She settles for handing her a tissue instead.*

May (*sobs*)   I can't believe this is happening again!

Penny   What's happening again, sweetie?

Ted   Here we go . . . Get over it already!

May   I AM over it!

Ted   Patently. It's been eighteen years! Move on! Look at me – I have! I've got a thriving dental practice, a big house, a beautiful wife –

Jacob   Oh yeah. What's her name again? The rich bitch. Sally? Sandy?

Ted   Susan.

Jacob   Susan! That's right.

He smirks at **Penny** *and swigs more baijiu.*

Penny *clears throat uncomfortably.*

Ted   The point is I moved on, worked hard and achieved something with my life. Something I can be proud of.

May (*cruelly*)   Like those medals on the ground over there?

Jacob   Yeah, no one gives a shit, Ted. So what happened eighteen years ago anyway? Why does she keep going on about it?

Penny *shrugs, genuinely baffled.*

May   The *chair*?!

She points at the plastic chair amongst the oak dining set.

Jacob   Yeah. It's an ugly piece of shit. And?

May   Penny?

Penny *and* **Jacob** *shrug at one another.*

Ted   Seriously, guys?

May *bursts into angry incoherent words/sobbing.*

Jacob   What?

Penny   May, sweetie, we can't understand you.

May *sobs harder.*

Ted (*sighs*)   *A mah* was watching some cooking programme and got it into her head that she'd bake a cake. Her first British cake. Her first time using the oven, probably. You guys had already moved out by then, but she invited everyone back. Wanted us all to have her real British cake.

Jacob   Oh, May. That must have been awful for you. *A mah* baked you a cake?

May *cries harder.*

Ted   Well, the recipe turned out to be harder than it looked, and it didn't turn out perfectly . . .

Penny (*to* May)   Oh no. You didn't say something to her, did you?

Anthony   Why? Why not?

Penny   Your *poh poh* wasn't always the best with criticism . . .

Ted   There's an understatement.

May   I was just a child! I didn't know! I didn't know how she used to get! One moment we were all chatting, laughing, eating cake, and all I said was that there was too much frosting, and then she'd broken a chair over my head.

Penny (*gasps*)   Oh, May . . .

May   She was shouting the most terrible things at me. *Swearing.* You two managed to hold her back, but she was still screaming at me. Penny took me to A&E to get stitches. I didn't even realise how much I'd been bleeding until I –

Anthony   That is bullshit!

Penny   Anthony!

Anthony   *Poh poh* wouldn't do that!

May   Are you calling me a *liar*?

Anthony   *Poh poh* was nice! She wouldn't do that!

Jacob *and* **Ted** *burst out laughing.*

Jacob (*laughs*)   Oh, Arnold. You have no idea . . .

Anthony   It's Anthony!

May   How can you laugh right now?!

Jacob (*laughs*)   Do you have any idea what she used to do to the rest of us?

Ted (*laughs*)   You're basically as clueless here as Anthony!

May   I am not!

Anthony   *Poh poh* wouldn't do that! She wouldn't! Right, mum?

Penny   Guys? Come on . . .

Anthony You're lying!

May How dare you? How –! (*Takes a breath.*) You know what? It's OK. I *forgive* you. I *forgive* you and I *forgive* her.

Jacob Really? 'Cause you kind of just said that like 'I fucking-hate all of you'.

May SHUT UP! I *FORGIVE* you!

Jacob, **Ted** *and* **Anthony** *burst out laughing.*

Penny Guys, maybe just lay off her for a while?

May (*sobs*) Haven't I been through enough?

Jacob *abruptly stops laughing.*

Jacob What the fuck do you think you've been through? You're a fucking American housewife! What do you know about suffering?

May I've been through just as much as you all have!

Her siblings all speak at once.

Ted / Oh, now that's obviously not true.

Penny Er . . . Well . . .

Jacob The fuck you have! You don't know the half of what the rest of us have been through!

May I'm a part of this family too!

Ted You're the baby, May. You were too young to remember anything.

May I am not the baby!

Penny (*fondly*) Oh, May. You'll always be the baby to me.

May I am *not* the baby!

Ted Yes, you are. I was the baby, and then you came along, and suddenly you were the baby. Seven years old. I was adorable up to seven years old. Cheeky, even. Then suddenly, whoosh! Invisible.

May   I was the invisible one! You all had your little secrets and inside jokes. I had *nobody*. No one ever told me anything! Ever!

Penny   Oh, May . . .

Jacob   Oh, boo fucking hoo! I don't know why you're even here. I don't know why you even think you deserve any of this.

May   Oh. So *that's* what all this was about? You're saying you deserve more than the rest of us?

Everyone turns and looks at **Jacob**.

Jacob   I do. I'm the oldest. I've been through way more than the rest of you.

Ted   Seriously?

Jacob   Hey – I was in *prison*!

Ted   Because you were dealing crack!

Jacob   I was dealing *meth*. There's a difference, OK?

Ted   Oh, well I beg your pardon!

Jacob   I *forgive* you.

Ted   Ha ha.

Jacob   Look, I've been through shit you guys couldn't even imagine.

May   As if. You were always was *a mah*'s favourite.

Ted   Well, I don't know about that. I rather think I was –

Jacob   She still hit me! And *a bah* had it out for me! The shit he used to do to me?

Penny   Guys. Let's not dwell on –

Jacob   And you. (*Laughs bitterly.*) Oh, you got it easy, didn't you, Penny?

Ted   Hey now. . .

Jacob   *A bah* never laid a finger on his precious Penny.
Never.

(*To* **Anthony**.) Your mum got everything.

Penny   I know. I did. I'm sorry.

Ted   Well, she got it extra bad from *a mah* though. (*Epiphany
moment.*) Hey – do you think that's why? Because Penny was
a bah's favourite?

Jacob   Of course that's why! (*To* **Anthony**.) Your mum got
everything when we were kids. Penny this. Penny that.

(*In Cantonese.*) Give it to Penny! Share with Penny!

Penny   I know. Your Uncle Jacob was very patient with me.

Ted   No he wasn't! He was horrible! To all of us!

Penny   But it is true. When *a bah* was still alive, I got it
easier than him. Than all of you. I'm sorry, guys. I am. I
know it wasn't fair. Especially to you, Jacob.

May   Don't apologise to him!

Ted   He was a bully! He made you pay several times over!
And so did *a mah*! Don't apologise!

Penny   But I am. I'm sorry.

Jacob (*to* **Anthony**)   I wasn't a bully. I was keeping this lot in
check, teaching them the order of things, teaching them
respect.

(*To his siblings.*) I mean, if we really kept score, I'd kick your
asses on the suffering scale. Each and every one of you.

Ted   Don't listen to him, Anthony.

May   There's no / way.

Jacob   It's true.

Ted   You didn't suffer financially, did you? Not like Penny and I.

Jacob   Oh, you want to really compare scores?

Ted *looks at* **Anthony***'s admiring face looking up at* **Jacob***.*

Ted   Yes, actually. I do. Let's do the maths, shall we?

Penny   Guys, this is silly. Let's just –

Ted   No. Come on. You're in this too, Penny.

Ted *rifles through a drawer, pulling out a pack of whiteboard markers.*

Penny   What are you –?

Ted   Anthony needs to know the truth! I'm going to explain – no, *prove* once and for all that Jacob is wrong.

Jacob   Tsch! Go ahead and try.

Ted *writes on a blank bit of wall: P O I N T S*

May   Are you crazy?! Those are permanent!

Ted   Not our house. Not our problem. Penny, you took care of *a mah* most of the last seven years. Let's say 100 points a year, that's fair, right?

Penny   I –

Ted *writes: 1 0 0 p t s / y e a r*

Jacob (*enjoying this*)   This is fucked up, man. . .

Ted   Anthony – take over.

Anthony   W-what? No. I don't –

Ted *throws* **Anthony** *the marker.* **Anthony** *stands by the wall, a Chinese teen boy Carol Vorderman, ready to write the numbers.*

Ted   We've both been sending her money, paying for things – so what shall we say? Ten points per hundred quid? How much do you reckon you've given her over the years?

Penny   Ted, I don't really want to –

Ted   You getting this, Anthony?

Anthony   Yeah.

Anthony *writes: 1 0 p t s / £ 1 0 0*

Ted   Five thousand a year . . . I'd say I've given her 40–50 grand? Not to mention the cruise and the gifts . . .

Jacob   This is bullshit, guys.

Ted   How about you, Pen? Twenty? Thirty grand? (*To* **Anthony**.) Just put three thousand.

May   Well what about me?

Jacob   / Shut up, May.

Ted   What about you?

May   She broke a chair over my head! That's 500 points. At least!

Jacob   Yeah, but you got piano lessons.

Ted   That's true. None of the rest of us got those.

May   Are you kidding me?! What does that have to do with –

Jacob   Who do you think was helping *a mah* pay for those while these two here were 'studying'? Hey, transfer those 500 points to me.

May   I didn't even want those stupid lessons! I *hated* them! She was the one who wanted me to take them! None of you know what I went through! Anthony – 100 points each grade I did for piano. A thousand points for the piano lessons and *600* points for the chair! As *compensation*!

Jacob   Compensation? Oh, we're doing 'compensation' now?

Penny   Guys, let's just stop and –

May   Yeah. We are.

Jacob   Oh, I am *so* going to win this. OK. Let's say bruises – twenty-five points. Each time she drew blood – fifty. Fractures or loss of consciousness – 100. I mean, the standard monthly beatings were probably just fifty points or so, but the big ones, you know, those happened what – once every two years? I'd give me 400 for each, easy.

Anthony *hesitates, pen in hand.*

Jacob   Keep up, Albert.

May   What are you even talking about?

Jacob   Oh yeah! And sometimes her memory was so bad from all the drinking and black outs she'd forget she already hit me once, and do it again just in case. Double points!

Ted   Ha! She used to do that to me too.

May   I don't remember this. Penny? What are they talking / about?

Penny   I –

Jacob   Of course you don't remember. You're the baby.

May   Stop calling me that!

Ted   By the time you were old enough to remember anything, most of us were too old for her to punish.

Anthony   Punish?

Ted   Well, in any sort of physical capacity anyway.

Penny   Although . . . (*Giggles.*) Remember the time in the car when she gave me that nosebleed. . .

Ted (*laughs*)   I'd forgotten about / that!

Jacob   Oh yeah! And the only thing we had in the car was that – that Happy Meal toy – what were those things?

Ted   Baby bear – no, baby . . .?

Penny   Beanie Baby!

Jacob (*laughs*)   Right! And you sat there with a fucking beanie baby / shoved up your nose!

Penny   Up my nose! (*Laughs.*) I did! I did!

Ted (*laughing*)   Wasn't it a lobster?

Penny (*nods, laughing*)   One claw up each nostril!

Jacob *mimes shoving a tiny lobster claw up each nostril.*

Jacob   Waaa-ah-ah . . . (*Stuff stuff.*) Aaahhhh . . .

Penny *and* **Ted** *laugh harder.*

Ted (*laughing*)   Surprisingly absorbent!

May   Was I there? How old was I?

Jacob   Duh. It was your toy. Why would the rest of us be having a Happy Meal?

Anthony *throws down the pen.*

Anthony   ENOUGH! I don't want to hear this anymore!

Penny *puts out a hand to soothe him, but he shakes it off.*

Anthony   You're talking about someone else! *Poh poh* wouldn't do that!

Jacob   Ha!

Ted   She did.

Penny *reluctantly nods.*

Anthony   But . . . then . . . how can you just – just *laugh* about it? Like it's – it's *normal*?

Jacob (*shrugs*)   'Cause it was. For us.

Penny   It's been so long, and . . . I mean, she was our mum. She raised us, made us dumplings, made us laugh . . . Sorry. I – I'm probably not explaining this right.

Ted   Allow me.

Jacob *and* **May** *roll their eyes.*

Ted   You see, Anthony, in this world, no one's really all good or all bad. Most of us are a bit of / both and –

Jacob (*big yawn*)   Forget it, Adrian.

Anthony   Anthony.

Jacob   Your mum's probably never hit you in your life has she?

Anthony   Of course not. That's child abuse.

Jacob   Yeah. If you're *British*. And I know you were born here, blah blah blah, but I mean British like your parents were born here, and your grandparents, and your grandparents' grandparents. Us? We're different.

Penny   Jacob, that's not true. Don't tell him that.

Anthony   No, I want to know. Why?

Jacob   Because we're the children of immigrants. Hell – you're lucky! Your mum spent most of her life here – that's why you've never gotten slapped. All of us (*indicating his siblings*) were raised by a real, proper, fresh off the boat immigrant – someone who came from a next-level shit situation in another country – and we had the shit beaten out of us, because you know what the thing is about immigrant parents?

Anthony *shakes his head.*

Jacob   They want you to be happy, but not that happy.

Anthony   What are you even talking about?

Jacob   They come here at great cost and sacrifice everything so that you'll have the opportunities they never had . . . but they never let you forget it. Maybe they genuinely think they mean well, but deep down on some sub-conscious level shit how could they not resent us? We have it so much better than them! So much! So that's why they smack us around a little bit.

Ted   Or a lot.

Jacob   That's right. Your *poh poh* resented the shit out of us whether she knew it or not. And you know who she resented most?

Anthony *shakes his head.*

Jacob   Your mum. Her first daughter. The girl who got everything she never had.

Penny   Well, I mean, it's not as simple as that.

Ted   That's right. You have to look at our historic, cultural and socio-economic context in which mental health wasn't really –

Jacob   Fuck mental health! She didn't need some shrink! She had this! (*Holds up the baijiu.*) You can't keep dwelling on the past when you're blackout drunk, can you?

Penny *looks thoughtfully at the bottle. She stands and heads to the dining table.*

Jacob   You ever had a drink, Ansel? It's fucking amazing.

Ted   Don't encourage a minor to drink!

May (*to* **Penny**)   Where are you going?

Penny   Her blackouts . . . I just . . .

Penny *gets to the plastic fold out chair and flips it over.*

May   What are you doing?!

Taped to the bottom is an envelope. **Penny** *tears it open revealing a stack of cash.*

Jacob   Holy shit.

Anthony   Whoa. Mum! You did it! You found the cash!

May   Some of it. That's not a lot.

Ted   How did you know?

Penny   I didn't. I just thought – Well, you found that other cash with her booze, and *a mah* was drinking so much and blacking out – her memory wasn't great – and well, I just figured she must've hidden the cash somewhere . . . memorable.

Ted   Places with a strong emotional connection. Of course!

May (*triumphant*)   Like the chair.

Jacob   Well, what are we waiting for?! Think! Go!

The siblings spring into action, scattering in different directions. **Jacob** *to the kitchen.* **May** *to the piano.* **Ted** *to his box of crushed awards.* **Penny** *pauses, then heads upstairs.*

Anthony *watches* **Ted** *rifling through his awards.*

Anthony   It doesn't look like there's anything there. Uncle Ted?

Ted   It'll be here. I mean, she was so proud of me. Always was . . .

May *waves a frayed bamboo feather duster and fat envelope from the piano.*

May   Two thousand! I found two thousand pounds!

Jacob   Dammit!

Ted *and* **Jacob** *continue their searches more vigorously.* **Anthony** *approaches* **May**.

Anthony   . . . What happened to the end of that duster?

May (*calmly ignores him*)   We spent hours at this piano. Do you play, Anthony?

Anthony   Yeah. But I don't really like practicing.

May   That's because you're not talented.

Anthony   Oh.

May   I was talented.

May *holds up the duster, inspecting the frayed end thoughtfully.*

May   She made me play four hours a day. Two before school. Two before bed.

She suddenly THWAPS the duster hard on the keys! **Anthony** *jumps.*

May   I'm the accompanist for our church choir. I only play for Jesus now.

She smiles, but it doesn't reach her eyes.

Ted   Aha! Why didn't I think of it before? Anthony – Give me a hand?

Ted *runs over to the shelf of various porcelain, wooden and crystal animals.* **Anthony** *joins him.*

Ted   Your Aunt Susan and I picked up the first one for her on our honeymoon. We just sort of kept up the tradition every time we went on holiday. It's a sort of inside joke we have. 'What pet will we bring back *a mah* this time?'

Ted *picks each one up carefully and looks under the base. He checks under the shelves and pats around.* **Anthony** *tries a few.*

Anthony   There's a lot of them.

Ted   A veritable menagerie. Susan and I have been together a long time. Fourteen years. Almost as long as you've been alive!

Anthony   Whoa.

Ted   I always say I'm the luckiest man in the world. Not everyone gets to marry their first love.

Jacob (*bursts out laughing*)   You married the woman who popped your cherry? God, you're pathetic.

Ted   Laugh all you want. I'm a proud romantic.

Jacob   Pfft! You don't think I'm romantic?

Ted   You've been divorced five times.

Jacob   Had to get married five times first though, didn't I?

Ted *has searched each figurine and is starting over again.*

Anthony   I don't think there's anything –

Ted   No, no. She's probably just hidden it somewhere clev–

Jacob   Ta da!

Jacob *places a tub of rat poison proudly on the counter. He opens the tub and pulls out an envelope.*

May   Is that . . . rat poison? Why would it be in there?

Jacob   You guys don't remember this?

Ted *and* **May** *give one another blank looks.*

Jacob   You were there! Oh, come on. There's a photo and everything!

Jacob *rifles through the shelves looking for the photo.*

Ted   Careful with the animals!

He's not.

Jacob (*shouts upstairs*)   Pen?! Where's that photo of us in those outfits?! Pen?!

(*To* **Anthony**.) Yo, Alex. Go find your mum for me.

Anthony   Anthony.

Penny *comes down the stairs holding an old book from which some envelopes stick out.*

Penny   Was someone shouting for me? I'm keeping an eye on the clock. We –

Jacob   Oi, where's that photo of – Nevermind! Found it!

He takes a framed photo off the shelf, knocking over one of **Ted's** *animals.* **Ted** *reaches out and rights it carefully.*

Jacob *shows them the photo.*

Anthony (*bursts out laughing*)   Is that you guys?! How old were you?

May   Oh my gosh. We look awful. Ted especially.

Ted   It's the glasses.

Jacob   It's the face.

Anthony *snaps a picture of the photo with his phone.*

Penny   Anthony!

Anthony   Nuh-uh. I'm posting it. The world needs to see this.

Ted   When *was* this photo taken?

(*To* **Jacob**.) You're still in it, so we must've all been pretty young.

Jacob   You really don't remember do you?

Ted *and* **May** *look blankly at him.*

Penny (*quietly*)   I do.

Jacob   Ted pissed the bed for weeks after.

Ted   Wait, what? I never –

Anthony (*laughing*)   Uncle Ted was a bedwetter?

Jacob   A big one. Teddy, Teddy wet the beddy!

Ted   No, I didn't! Stop it!

Jacob   Teddy, Teddy wet the –

May   So what happened?

Penny (*in Cantonese to* **Jacob**)   Let's not tell them . . .

Jacob (*in Cantonese*)   What does it matter?

Ted   We can all understand Cantonese, you know.

May   Yeah.

Anthony   I don't.

Penny (*sigh*)   It was just a normal school night, but she made us all put on our nicest clothes.

Anthony   Those were your nicest clothes?

Ted, **May** *and* **Jacob** *glare at him. He shuts up.*

Penny   We'd only been in London a year or so, because I remember we were all homesick, so she went out to Chinatown and got all of our favourite foods: (*In Cantonese.*) pig ears, crab, custard buns . . .

Jacob   Those little dessert things! *Tong yoon!*

May (*wrinkles nose*)   Too much sugar.

Penny   Then we all we sat down for dinner, and you two (**Ted** *and* **May**) were beyond excited. You guys were so young. You just thought it was New Year or something.

Jacob   We knew better though, huh?

Penny   Well, maybe you did, but I wasn't sure. I thought maybe we were celebrating something, but she wasn't telling us . . .?

Anthony   So, were you guys?

Penny   We finished eating. We were so full, we could hardly move. That's when she told us to stand together for the photo. 'Smile! *Siu duk hoi sum dee la!*'

Anthony   Uh, English please?

Penny   'Big happy smiles! They can use this in the papers. Then they'll know we were a happy family.'

May   The papers?

Penny   That's what I asked. 'Yes. When we're all dead.' Then she showed us that tub of rat poison. 'I put it in everything,' she said. 'Sprinkled it like salt. We'll be dead in the morning.' Then she made us all brush our teeth and comb our hair – she did yours for you, May – two little French braids – and sent us to bed. She told us they'd find us in our pretty outfits and not to be scared. (*In Cantonese.*) 'No need to be scared. Sleep well!'

Ted But – I don't remember any of this!

Jacob Your bed does. (*Mimes pee spraying out of* **Ted**'s *crotch.*)

Ted Stop it!

Jacob *laughs*.

May I think I might I remember the –

Jacob Shut up, May. You were still in nappies.

May So? I have a very good memory, you know! I –

Jacob Man, I didn't sleep a wink that night.

Penny Me neither.

Anthony But you're not dead . . . So it was all a joke? Why would she do that?!

Jacob It's pretty funny when you think about it in hindsight.

Ted No, it's not! It's horrible!

May I can't believe I went through all of that trauma.

Jacob Whatever, May! You didn't have a clue what was going on! For all you knew we were at fucking Disneyland!

May (*tragically*) I've never been to Disneyland.

Penny I don't know if it was a joke. I mean, now in retrospect . . . I think she might've genuinely thought it would work. *A bah* was dead. She was in a new country, and we were all so young. I don't think she was coping very well.

Anthony Why did she stay? Why didn't she just go back home then?

Jacob Alright, Nigel Farage. Calm down.

Penny   She did it for us. Everything. She wanted to stay and give us a new life. A better one than she had.

May   Wait. So why didn't we die then?

Penny   Maybe she just didn't put enough in?

Jacob   Y'know, some junkie once told me that most rat poison is 97 per cent food and only 3 per cent poison.

Anthony   Is that true?

Jacob (*shrugs*)   Meh. Beats me, but it's a good business model if what you're selling is the poison.

Ted   It was probably just a bad batch. Knowing *a mah*, she probably got it at some dodgy pound shop.

He lifts the tub up and looks on the bottom.

Ted   Ha! There. You see? 99p!

Penny *tries not to, but a giggle escapes.*

May   What is wrong with you? Our mother tried to kill us!

Penny (*laughing*)   Sorry! It's just – It wasn't even a pound! She got it at a 99p shop!

Penny *continues laughing.* **Jacob** *joins in first. Then* **Ted**.

Jacob (*laughing*)   She was going to be dead!

Ted (*laughing*)   And she was still trying to get a bargain!

They're laughing so hard they can barely speak. **May** *gives a reluctant smile.*

May   She did like saving money, didn't she? She used to take all those extra napkins from fast food places . . .

Penny (*laughing and nodding*)   There's still some in that drawer over there!

May *finally joins in the laughter.*

May (*laughing*)   Oh gosh! I don't know why I'm laughing! This is really sad!

Ted (*laughing*)   We're so going to hell to for this!

May (*laughing*)   You're all going anyway!

This sets them off again.

Anthony   You guys are so weird. . .

As he waits for their laughing fit to pass, he notices his mother's finds from upstairs and reaches for them. **Jacob** *instantly snaps. The mood changes.*

Jacob   Hey! That's not yours!

Anthony   I was just looking.

Jacob   Well don't! Hands off!

Penny   Jacob, he didn't mean anything.

Jacob *pulls three envelopes out of the old book in* **Penny**'s *hands. He shoves them at* **May**.

Jacob   Count them. May counts the money.

Ted   You found *three*? I haven't even found one . . .

May   Where'd you find these?

Penny   Oh, you guys don't want to hear all that.

Jacob   I do. I knew every spot up there. There's no way I missed something.

Jacob *gives her a warning look.*

Penny   Well, um, that one was in *a bah*'s urn.

May *gingerly sets down the envelope, takes out some hand sanitiser, and uses it.*

Penny   That one was in that box of old extension cables, and this one – (*In Cantonese.*) This was in her old diary.

Ted   *A mah* had a diary?

Ted *eyes the book in* **Penny**'*s hand. She hugs it closer to herself.*

Jacob (*to* **May**)   Oi, hurry up. How much is that?

Anthony   What happened with the extension cables?

Penny   It's really not much of a story.

Anthony   I wanna know.

Penny   She'd just use them for discipline. So, that's all of it, right? We can divide it now?

Anthony   No, no – hold up. *Poh poh* used to discipline you guys with extension cables? Like whip you guys?

Ted   Just your mum, I think.

The other siblings nod in agreement.

Anthony   What? Why? How is that fair?

Penny   It wasn't – I mean, I –

Anthony   How old were you?

Penny   It doesn't matter.

Anthony   How old were you?

Penny   . . . I guess the last time was when I was about your age? Maybe a bit older? Sixteen?

Anthony   Why didn't you stop her?! I'd never let anyone do that to me! Never!

Penny   I guess – I guess I felt like it was the least I could do for her.

Anthony   For what?! What could you possibly owe her?

Penny *fidgets with her mother's diary.*

Penny   She was my mother.

Anthony   So?! I'd never let you do that to me.

May   Maybe she should. Teach you some manners.

Anthony Oh, please. I –

Penny Because her parents did far worse to her. I just – No matter how bad things got with her, I always remembered that she had it so much worse. Her parents took . . . so much from her, and she still managed to give so much to us.

Ted *takes the diary from* **Penny**.

Ted What's in this thing?

Penny No! Don't –

Ted *holds it out of her reach.*

Ted It's fine. I probably won't be able to read half of it anyway. My Chinese is pretty rusty.

Penny Jacob! Stop him!

Jacob (*in Cantonese*) If he wants to, then let him.

Penny But –!

May Shh! Guys, I'm trying to concentrate here.

Anthony But mum! MUM! You just let her whip you because she had a crappy life back in Hong Kong or wherever? I mean, that has nothing to do with you!

Penny How could it not? She was my mother. She raised me.

May £15,000! We're at £15,000.

Jacob Shit! We're still missing five grand?! How much time do we have before the funeral?

Penny Well, we should get there early and–

Ted (*gasp*) Oh . . . no . . . Oh no . . . Oh –

Jacob Congrats. You found it, didn't you?

Ted I'm gonna be sick.

Ted *drops the diary, runs to the bin and heaves.*

Ted No wait. I'm not. No wait. I am. (*Dry heaves.*)

Penny   Sorry! I tried to warn you, Ted! I –

May   Ugh. He's making me feel a bit sick now. Will someone please tell me what's going on?

Anthony   And me.

Penny   No.

Anthony   But Mu-um! I've already heard everything else!

Jacob   Trust your mum on this one, Antoine. OK, focus, guys. Where's the other five grand?

May   Well at least tell *me*. I've got just as much of a right to know as you guys! Ted?

Ted *dry retches, then looks like he might cry.*

Penny   Shh. It's OK . . .

Ted   How long? How long have you guys known?

Jacob   Oh ages.

May   Known what? Tell me!

Penny   She told me when I turned thirteen.

Jacob   Oh yeah. That makes sense. I don't know. I was probably fifteen or sixteen? She used to get drunk and talk about it.

May   Talk about what? Guys! This isn't fair! I'm a part of this family too!

Jacob   Sure, baby May. First, / we've got to find the –

May   Don't call me th–!

Ted *charges at* **Jacob**. **Jacob** *easily dodges him and pushes him back.*

Jacob   What the fuck?!

Penny   / Ted!

May   What is happening?!

Ted   HOW COULD YOU?! How could you know this and still – still treat her the way you did?! The way you're still treating her!

Jacob   What do you mean?

Ted   All you do is take and take and take!

Jacob   I don't –

Ted   Hadn't she had enough taken from her? I mean, look around! Look what we've done to her house!

Jacob   Hey, this isn't on me, man. You're the one who went all Banksy on her walls.

Ted   How many times did she bail you out? Pay for your lawyers? Lend you money?

Jacob   So?

Ted   Your five divorces – Those weren't cheap!

Jacob   Well, if she'd raised a better son, maybe they wouldn't have left me.

Ted   Stop! Just stop! I did EVERYTHING she ever wanted, but did she confide in me? NO! She told you! She trusted you! She told you about her hidden stashes! She told you about her childhood! Look around this room! It's all you! Where do you see any of the rest of us?! She loved *you*! And you treated her like shit!

Jacob *looks in silence at the various photos in the room.*

Ted   Yeah! That's right! I hope I'm finally getting through that thick, self-centred skull of yours!

Jacob   Hold that thought . . . I've got five photos in here, but you know who has more?

Jacob *picks up a school photo of* **Anthony**.

Anthony   Hey! Put that down!

May   One, two, three, four . . . There's seven! She's got seven photos of Anthony!

Anthony   So? Mum sends her my school photos.

Penny   I mean, if you don't send it to their grandparents what else are you supposed to do with them, right?

Tries to laugh it off.

Ted   I had school photos. I don't see any of them up.

May   You don't see Emma or Kelly's photos either, do you? She always preferred sons over daughters. Of course she'd be the same with grandchildren.

Jacob   Where's the other five grand, Ashley?

Anthony (*getting nervous*)   Mum?

Penny   Shh. It's alright, honey. He doesn't know where the money is! How could he? He's just a kid.

Jacob   *You* said he was her only male grandchild. *You* said she doted on him.

Penny   This is ridiculous! . . . Right? Ted?

Ted   I – I don't – I don't know. Now I'm not so sure . . .

Jacob   All I'm saying is, Archibald here's been pretty calm about this whole thing.

Anthony   I don't want to get involved in all this stupid drama, OK?

Jacob   I mean, twenty thousand pounds? When I was his age, my brain would've exploded if someone offered me half that!

Ted   I hate to say this, but Jacob does have a point. We've all been running around and Anthony's just been sitting there on his phone.

Penny   He's a teenager.

Anthony   I was sitting here because I – I don't know where to look! I've never lived here! I don't have any bad memories of *poh poh* – not like you guys!

May   But you have memories of her, right?

Anthony *hesitates.*

May   Go on. You can tell your Auntie May. What do you remember about your *poh poh*?

Penny   Guys, don't do this! Honey, you don't have to answer them.

Jacob   No. He does. Where's the money, Alfie? Stop being difficult.

Anthony   I'm not! And it's Anthony! You can't even get my fucking name right!

Penny   Anthony! / Jacob, he –

Jacob   Are you talking back to me?

Anthony *lowers his gaze.*

Anthony   . . . No.

Jacob   Hey! I'm your elder and I'm talking to you! Look at me! I said, are you talking back to me?

Anthony   No

Jacob   When I was your age, you know what my dad used to do if I talked back to my elders?

Penny   Jacob . . .

Jacob   Hey! I asked you a question! Do you know what my dad used to do if I talked back to my elders?

Anthony   No. No, I don't know.

Jacob   He'd smack me across the mouth. Then he'd keep smacking and smacking until my mouth was so swollen, I couldn't talk. The only thing soft enough to eat all week would be congee. But he was right – you don't forget to respect your elders after that . . . I fucking hate congee. So let's try this again – what memories do you have of your *poh poh*?

Anthony   She – She was always cooking, but like, it's not a big deal or anything.

Ted   Maybe he really doesn't kn–

Jacob   What did she cook?

Anthony   I dunno! . . . Dumplings?

Ted   Ah yes, I loved her dumplings.

Jacob   Shut up, Ted. And?

Anthony   And I told her I didn't like prawns, so she used to make pork ones just for me. I loved watching her make them. She had that green marble rolling pin and she was so fast but – but they were all so perfect. Each one was exactly the same. And when she finally ran out of stuffing, she'd take the leftover dough and –

Jacob   – make it into a little bird just for you.

Anthony   How did you know?

Jacob   She used to do that for me too.

Ted   What? She never did that for me!

May   That's because you weren't her favourite.

Beat.

Ted (*sputters*)   Well . . . I – I mean . . .

Jacob *tackles* **Anthony**.

Anthony   / NO!

Penny   No! Stop!

Jacob   Help me hold him down! What are you waiting for? Ted!

Ted *hesitates just a beat, then helps* **Jacob** *hold* **Anthony.** **Penny** *tries to pull them off, but she's outnumbered.*

Jacob   May! The kitchen! Check the drawer with the rolling pin!

May *runs to the kitchen and dumps out the drawer. She grabs up an envelope, triumphant.*

May   It's here! There's . . . a few grand! At least!

Jacob   Keep talking, kid.

Anthony   No! I swear I don't know. She didn't tell me anything!

Penny   He doesn't know anything! Jacob! (*In Cantonese.*) He really doesn't know anything!

Jacob   May! Go grab that box of extension cables from upstairs.

May *runs upstairs.*

Anthony   Why? Why do you need those? What are you going to do?

Penny   Let him go!

Jacob *leaves* **Anthony** *to* **Ted** *and grabs* **Penny**'*s arms.*

Penny   Jacob!

May *runs back with the box of cables.*

Ted (*nervously*)   Jacob? What are we doing here?

Jacob   Calm down. We're just tying them up. Move them to the dining chairs.

Anthony   Uncle Jacob, please! Don't do this!

Jacob   Pass me that. No. The other one.

Jacob, May *and* **Ted** *tie* **Anthony** *and* **Penny** *to two of the dining chairs with the extension leads.*

Penny   Don't do this, guys! Just think about it! Why would *a mah* tell him?

Jacob (*at* **Penny**)   You, shut up!

(*At* **Anthony**.) You, talk!

Anthony   I don't know, OK?! I – Uh – Her exercise thingy! *Poh poh* used to let me play on it!

Jacob   What exercise thingy?

Ted   The elliptical trainer. I bought it for her. Susan made us get one for the spare room, and *a mah* saw it and wanted one too. Now let's see here . . .

Ted *starts to pull at one of the elliptical trainer's pedals.* **Jacob** *butts him out of the way and rips it apart.*

Jacob   There's nothing here!

Anthony   I don't know, OK?! She didn't tell me anything!

Jacob *raises a fist.*

Penny   No! You will *not* hit my son.

Jacob   I will if he doesn't talk!

Anthony   Why are you doing this?!

Penny   Ted! May! Wake up! How do you think this is going to end, guys?! You're going to find all the money and then Jacob's just going to split it with you and walk away? When has he ever played fair?! When has he ever done anything that wasn't the most self-serving, self-centred, easy way ou–

Jacob *slaps* **Penny**.

Ted   Jacob!

Anthony   The armchair! She told me I could have her favourite chair! But she didn't mention any money! I swear!

Jacob   Now was that so bad?

Jacob *grabs a kitchen knife and slices open the chair.* **May** *steps toward the armchair to help.* **Jacob** *holds out the knife.*

Jacob   Uh uh – Not so fast.

May   Ha! You're not going to stab me.

Ted   May, just do as he says.

May (*laughs*)   Don't be ridiculous!

Penny *and* **Ted** *look dead serious.*

May (*still incredulous*)   What?

Penny   Jenny – his third wife . . .

Ted   *She* caught *him* cheating. Apparently he just missed her heart by few millimetres.

Jacob   Aw, you remembered!

Anthony (*at* **Penny**)   But you said –

Jacob   She said I didn't stab anyone *in prison*. Always protecting me, aren't you, Pen?

Jacob *never takes his eyes off them as he feels around for the envelope.*

Jacob   Hey, if it makes you feel better, she hit me first, OK? And to be fair, I was cheating on her with my fourth wife, so really, I did it out of love.

He finds the envelope and smiles.

Jacob   That was the first time *a mah* lied for me in court. I guess I do have some good memories of her.

He blows a kiss at the portrait.

Jacob   *A mah* . . .

He swipes all of the cash, jewellery and valuables into a biscuit tin and heads for the door.

Ted   Oh come on, Jacob. You don't have to be so predictably dickish.

Jacob   I deserve this money.

May   Well, so do I!

Jacob *doubles over laughing, then suddenly flips to angry.*

Jacob   What the fuck do you think you guys deserve! I could've gone to university. I could've been a dentist just like you, or even – I don't know – a brain surgeon! But I didn't! I had to go out and work to support you guys!

Ted   You really are delusional . . . It wasn't because of us! You didn't go to university because it was hard work. It's easier to sell drugs than it is to actually sit down and study for something. Penny's right! You were always trying to find the easy way out! You're not the hero you think you are, Jacob! You're a wife beater and you treated *a mah* like your personal piggy bank! You made her perjure for you in court!

Jacob   I still went down!

Ted   Yeah, because you were guilty!

Jacob   She could've tried harder! Got me a better lawyer! Got my sentence reduced!

Ted   You always want more, don't you? *A mah* put up with things from you the rest of us would've never got away with! She gave you everything! And you're still just taking, taking, taking!

Jacob   How dare you speak to me like that? How dare you disrespect me like that?

Ted   Oh please. You and your respect. You're obsessed with it!

Jacob   You think you're all so good with your degrees and piano and shit? Let me ask you this – All of you. Who do you think truly respects you?

Ted   A lot of people. I'll have you know I've got a team of 15 people working for me – associates, assistants, hygienists. . .

Jacob   I don't mean who works for you. I mean who *respects* you. I walk into a room and people *know*. They don't know they know, but they do. They feel it right up here – (*Pokes* **Ted***'s forehead.*) and right down here. (*Pokes at* **Ted***'s groin.*)

Ted *bats* **Jacob***'s hand away.*

Ted   Stop it!

Jacob   Respect is making someone's asshole clench and their testicles SLLLURP right in because you're in the room. You ever make anyone do that?

Ted   What? No! I mean, Yes! I mean – You know what I mean! Probably.

Jacob   Probably? Probably? Oh Ted. Teddy Ted Ted. You're worse than I thought. How 'bout you, May? You ever made anyone SLLLUUUURP!

May   Don't be disgusting. Besides, I get plenty of respect, thank you. I am a mother, / and a –

Jacob   Penny? Actually, why am I even asking? Of course not. Look at that piece of shit husband you had. (*Aside to* **Anthony**.) Sorry, kid, but he was.

Penny   I think what you're talking about isn't respect. I think it's fear.

Jacob   You're damn right it is. How do you guys not know this? *A mah* knew it. It's how she raised us. Maybe we weren't the happiest of kids, but we sure as hell respected her.

(*To* **Ted**.) So, yeah. That's what I'm talking about. Respect. When people see me, they know I'm somebody, OK? I'm like a great white shark! I'm fucking Jaws, and you're . . . (*Laughs.*) Bambi. Dead mum and all. Look at you. Who wants you? Who wants to be *you*?

Jacob *turns to go.*

Ted   You know, you may have *a mah's* money, and you may even have been her favourite, but you will never, NEVER have my respect.

Jacob *stops in his tracks.*

Penny (*in Cantonese*)   Jacob, don't! Don't do it! (*Back to English.*) You've won already! You've got the money! Just go!

Ted   I'm not scared of you. You're a pathetic, ex-con, loser nobody who –

Jacob *puts his lips to* **Ted**'s *ear.*

Jacob   I. Fucked. Susan.

Ted   W-What?

Jacob   Your wife. I fucked her. And she loved it.

Ted   You're lying. You're making this up just like you always do for everything.

Jacob   Why don't you ask Penny? Go on.

Ted   No. I'm not going to because –

Penny   Ted . . . I didn't know how to . . . I'm sorry.

Ted (*tearful*)   When?

Jacob (*laughs*)   Which time?

Penny   Jacob, stop . . .

Jacob   You're not even your wife's favourite.

Beat. **Ted** *starts to cry.*

Jacob   Are you actually crying? Fuck, you really are pathetic, aren't you? (*Laughs.*) You've worked your whole damn life to get all these achievements, these accomplishments, to sound like the smartest guy in every room, and for what?

Jacob *grinds his heel into* **Ted***'s box of awards on the ground.*

Jacob   You'll never be anyone's favourite. I've won. Just like I've always won. You're nothing. You're no one.

Ted *weeps.*

Jacob (*chants*)   Teddy Teddy wet the beddy . . . Teddy Teddy wet the beddy . . .

Jacob *picks up a mug of cold tea and pours it over* **Ted***'s crotch.*

Jacob   Teddy Teddy wet the beddy . . .

Ted *weeps.*

Jacob   Say it with me. (*Chants.*) Teddy Teddy wet the beddy . . .

Penny   No. Don't do this, Ted. Don't listen to him!

Beat.

Ted (*weakly*)   Teddy Teddy wet the beddy . . .

Jacob (*whispers*)   That's right. Now what are you?

Ted   I'm nothing.

Beat.

Ted *dries his eyes.*

Ted   I'm going to go now.

Penny *opens her mouth to protest.*

Ted   No, Penny. It's OK. I don't need my share of *a mah*'s money. I never had a share of her anyway.

Ted *exits.*

Jacob (*snores, then snorts awake*)   Oh good. He's done. Well, I'm off too.

May   But –! But you can't!

Jacob   Aw, is widdle May gonna cry 'cause I took all her money-woney?

Jacob *gathers his things and turns to go.*

Jacob *(laughs)*   Don't be such a *baby.*

May   I said, DON'T CALL ME THAT!

May *grabs a dining chair and breaks it over* **Jacob***'s head.* **Jacob** *crumples to the ground.*

Anthony   / Holy shit!

Penny   May!

May *looks at them for a shocked beat, then grabs the biscuit tin of money, opens her suitcase and jams it in.*

Penny   May, what are you / doing? May!

Anthony   Hey! At least untie us!

May *ignores them and continues cramming in the money.*

Jacob *moans.*

May *freezes.*

Penny   Jacob! Are you OK?

Jacob*'s moan turns to a laugh.*

May   Why is he laughing like that? Oh God, I've damaged something, haven't I?

Jacob *laughs harder.*

Anthony   / Uncle Jacob?

Penny   Jacob? You're scaring me.

Jacob *howls with laugher.*

May   What are you –? Are you laughing *at me?*

Jacob *(laughing)*   Oh May . . . I did not see that one coming! How does it feel then?

May   How does what feel?

Jacob   Do you feel lighter? Do you feel your burdens floating away?

May   What are you talking about?

Jacob   You don't get to carry it around with you anymore!

May   What are you talking about? I don't carry what around with me anymore?

Jacob   The chair! Your thing that defines you. You're the girl whose mother hit her over the head with a chair.

May   I FORGAVE her!

Jacob   No you haven't. You hate her. You hate her and you love every second of it.

May   I –

Jacob   Look at you. You can't even deny it. You just carry around that hurt and that hate and feel so much better than the rest of us because what happened to you was so unfair! No one suffered as much as you! No one was as mistreated as you were! And now it's GONE because you've gone and done the exact same thing to me! Who are you now, May? You still think you deserve so much more than the rest of us?

May   I – Well –

Jacob   Look at her! So torn. Can't keep playing the poor little victim! You want to know suffering? That diary is suffering. Go ahead. Take it.

Penny   No! Jacob, don't –!

May   You know I can't read Chinese.

Jacob   Fine. Then I'll just tell you, shall I?

Penny (*in Cantonese*)   Jacob! Don't tell her the –

Jacob   *A mah* was thirteen and her father needed opium money so he whored her out. Stood right in the next room listening to her scream as some guy raped her. Didn't do a thing. What do you think about that? Still feel bad about your widdle wonely childhood?

Anthony *and* **May** *react together.*

May   / I – She –

Anthony   What? No!

Jacob   Or did you mean the time her mother burned her with sticks because she'd wet the bed? Or maybe the time both of her parents threw her in the dump when she was six? Thought she was dead. Some parasite or fever or something. That's what they did in those days. Threw their children on the side of the street with the rest of the rubbish. The village waste collector had to knock on their door, tell them she was still moving. 'Ugh, excuse me. Your baby girl's not quite dead. Can't take her. Soz.'

May (*angry*)   Why didn't you guys tell me?

Penny   I was protecting y –

Jacob (*shrugs*)   Never came up.

Anthony   You're a – a psychopath!

Jacob   Ha! (*Indicating* **May**.) Well if I am then she is too. You're not really upset, are you?

May   What are you talking about? Of course I'm –

Jacob   Not about what happened to *a mah*. You're just upset because of what it means for you.

May   What –

Jacob *thrusts the diary in* **May**'s *face.*

Jacob   This is what it feels like to be alone! This is suffering! This is fucked up! This is closer than you're ever going to get to being nailed up on some cross like your God! So go ahead. Do you still want to leave with *a mah's* money?

May *looks torn for a moment, then resolve sets in.*

May   Watch me.

May *slams shut her suitcase and zips it up. It won't close. She sits on the top and tries again.*

Jacob (*laughs*)   You do realise, of course, that if you take the money, you'll never have a reason to be mad at her again? Mad at us?

May *hesitates.*

Jacob (*laughs*)   You can't bear to take anything out of your baggage, can you?

Anthony   Just take the money and go! Don't let him have it!

Penny   May! Think of Emma and Kelly. Think of what it could do for them! Not just the money – They could have a mum – healed and whole! Don't you want that for them? Don't you want them to be happy?

May *freezes.*

Beat.

She takes the money out and sets it on the ground.

Anthony   / No! What are you doing?! You were so close!

Penny   May!

She zips up her case.

May   I'll see you at the service, Penny.

Penny   But –!

May   I'll find my own way there. I don't need your help. I don't need anyone's help.

Beat.

I think I will play the piano after all.

She hobbles with her case to the door, then turns and looks at the portrait of her mother.

May (*viciously*)   I *forgive* you.

Jacob (*laughing*)   Yeah, you fucking do . . .

May *smiles bitterly and leaves.* **Jacob** *heads for the money.*

Penny *and* **Anthony** *look at one another. With* **Jacob** *distracted, they struggle in their restraints.* **Anthony** *wriggles free first and stands.*

He holds out his phone and snaps a photo of **Jacob**. *At the camera click,* **Jacob** *spins around.*

Jacob   Why you little –!

Anthony   No! I'll call the cops! I'll do it!

Anthony'*s finger hovers over his phone.* **Jacob** *stops, his instinct of self-preservation wrestling with his rage.*

Jacob   What do you want, kid? You want me to split this with you? What do you say? 70/30? . . . 60/40?

Anthony *stands beside his mother, still untying herself from the extension leads, and holds her bruised cheek up to the light. He snaps a photo.*

Anthony   They're gonna know you stole *poh poh*'s money, tied us up, and hit my mum!

Jacob   I'm not giving you more, Alistair.

Anthony   Anthony! And I swear I'll post these photos if you don't give the money back right now! All of it!

Jacob   You're forgetting something.

Anthony   What? No I'm not.

Penny *stands and takes* **Anthony**'*s phone from him.*

Anthony   Mum? What are you doing? Mum!

Jacob (*in Cantonese*)   Penny loves her brother, doesn't she? (*In English.*) Good old Penny would never let you send her brother back to jail. Would you, Pen? No, she knows how to respect her elders.

Anthony   Mum!

Penny   I – I'm sorry.

Anthony (*confused, scared*)   Mum?

Jacob   When you're born in the year of the rat, you're gonna act like one. . .

Anthony   Shut up! Stop talking!

Jacob (*laughs*)   She's like a starving rat. So hungry for tiniest bit of love and approval she'll swallow it right down with the poison.

Penny (*tearfully*)   Sorry!

Anthony   Stop it!

Jacob   Your mum's the smartest of us all, you know. See – she knew from the start she was a worthless piece of shit. (*In Cantonese.*) A splat of shit. (*Back in English.*) That's why you're always apologising, isn't it Pen? Because you know you're nothing but a burden on the rest of us. 'Sorry! I'm so sorry! Sorryyy!'

Anthony   Shut up! Don't do this! Mum! Don't you dare delete those photos! Please, Mum!

Penny (*crying*)   I'm sorry. I'm sorry. I'm sorry . . .

She continues to apologise as she deletes the first photo.

Anthony   No! Don't! Stop apologising! You don't owe him anything! Don't delete it! Don't –!

She deletes the second photo.

Penny   I'm sorry. I'm so, so sorry.

Jacob   'Sorry! Sorry!' She can't help herself.

Jacob *grabs the box of money and limps to the door.*

Anthony   No! Mum! You can't let him get away with this! *Mum!*

Jacob (*in Cantonese*)   There's a good girl. (*Back in English.*) That, Anthony, is respect.

Jacob *exits.*

Anthony   WHY DID YOU DO THAT?! WHY DID YOU LET HIM TAKE *POH POH'S* MONEY?!

Penny   Because I don't deserve it.

Anthony   And what about me?! Don't I deserve it?! I could've put that toward, I don't know, driving lessons, or uni, or something! *Poh poh* wanted me to have that money!

Penny   She wanted you to have her chair. That was her favourite chair. Look at it now. It's destroyed. Everything's been destroyed.

Anthony   It's not my fault! They did it!

Penny   I'm making some tea. Do you want some tea?

Anthony   No! No I don't want your stupid tea! I want you to go out and get back *poh poh*'s money!

Penny *proceeds to make tea.*

Anthony   I hate you! You stupid, stupid bitch!

Penny (*calmly*)   Don't you *ever* feel it?

Anthony   Feel what?!

Penny   That overwhelming sense of guilt?

Anthony   For what?!

Penny   The things your *poh poh* went through, the things she sacrificed just so that we could have the things we have – doesn't that ever cross your mind? How are we ever supposed to *deserve* let alone repay that?

Anthony   I didn't ask for any of it!

Penny   Neither did I, but we live with the benefits anyway.

She hands him a cup of tea.

Penny   That money was everything she ever sacrificed to provide for us, and maybe Jacob was right. Maybe she resented us for it and was mean and selfish and didn't want us to be happy. And maybe May was right. Maybe your *poh poh* did this all on purpose. But if withholding it allowed her to die in peace, with no resentment to us, then I'm glad she did.

Anthony   You're talking absolute shit, Mum.

She ignores him as she continues her train of thought.

Penny   Maybe that's the inheritance she left us with. A chance at a fresh start. Don't you see? I don't owe her anything anymore. (*Delighted laugh.*) I don't owe her anything anymore!

Anthony   What the fuck are you talking about?! We just lost twenty thousand pounds and you're sitting here expecting me to drink tea?! I'm not going to fucking drink that!

Penny   OK. Then don't.

She swipes it off the table. It shatters on the ground.

Anthony   The fuck are you doing?!

Penny   You know what? I don't want tea either.

She drops hers too.

Anthony   Are you fucking insane?!

Penny   Don't you see it? I'm free! From now on, I drink what I want, when I want. (*Delighted gasp.*) I'll go get some wine. No! Champagne! I'll show up to her funeral tipsy! (*Laughs.*) Come on, honey. Let's escape this family together!

She grabs her keys and goes to pick up the portrait.

Give me a hand with this?

Slowly, calmly, **Anthony** *takes a breath and responds.*

Anthony   You just gave away twenty thousand pounds that *poh poh* probably meant to leave for me because I'm her favourite fucking grandchild. I think your brothers and sisters are all cunts, and I think you're the dumbest, stupidest *bitch* I ever met in my life.

He looks at his grandmother's portrait.

Anthony   I understand now. I understand everything. *Poh poh* was mean and selfish and didn't want you to be happy . . . and you're *just* like her.

Penny *slaps* **Anthony** *across the face.*

Penny   And I am NOT sorry!

Blackout.

End of Play.

For a complete listing of
Methuen Drama titles, visit:
www.bloomsbury.com/drama

Follow us on Twitter and keep up to date
with our news and publications
@MethuenDrama